75 YEARS OF
America's First Theme Park

JIM FUTRELL, RON GUSTAFSON, DAVE HAHNER, NELL HEDGE, and LEAH KOCH

an imprint of
INDIANA UNIVERSITY PRESS

This book is a publication of

Quarry Books
an imprint of
Indiana University Press
Office of Scholarly Publishing
Herman B Wells Library 350
1320 East 10th Street
Bloomington, Indiana 47405 USA

iupress.org

This book is printed on acid-free paper.

Manufactured in China

First Printing 2022

Cataloging information is available
from the Library of Congress.

ISBN 978-0-253-06289-5 (hdbk.)
ISBN 978-0-253-06290-1 (web PDF)

To three generations of visionaries who came before; may we honor your memory, grow beyond your wildest dreams, and see the next generation do the same.

Leah Koch

Contents

Acknowledgments

A book of this magnitude is not possible without the support of numerous individuals and organizations. The authors are grateful to the following:

Jim Futrell would like to thank Leah Koch, director of communications and fourth-generation owner, and Matt Blumhardt, vice president and chief operating officer at Holiday World & Splashin' Safari, for their vision and support in making this book a reality, along with attractions industry journalist Tim O'Brien for his encouragement and the other authors who were all so great to work with.

Ron Gustafson graciously thanks Holiday World & Splashin' Safari owners Lori and Leah Koch for sharing their incredible memories of family road trips that led to the development of the water park and sharing invaluable information related to the numerous expansion projects over the years. Thanks also to Lori Gogel, director of revenue administration, Holiday World & Splashin' Safari; and Phil Hayles, vice president business development and strategic accounts, ProSlide Technology, for their comments and technical data. Additional thanks to those who agreed to telephone interviews for the Recollections piece: John Wood, chairman and CEO, Sally Dark Rides/Sally Corporation; Rick Emmons, graphic artist, Holiday World & Splashin' Safari; Ed Janulionis, sales manager, Allan Herschell Company, North Tonawanda, New York; Tim O'Brien, amusement industry journalist; Eric Snow, vice president and chief marketing officer, Holiday World & Splashin' Safari; Don Baggett, magician, Holiday World & Splashin' Safari; Matt Blumhardt, vice president and chief operating officer, Holiday World & Splashin' Safari; Matt Eckert, president and chief executive officer, Holiday World & Splashin' Safari; Korey Kiepert, member/manager, The Gravity Group; DeeAnn Woolems, accounting manager, Holiday World & Splashin' Safari; and Rick Hunter, chairman and chief executive officer, ProSlide Technology.

Dave Hahner would like to thank numerous individuals at Holiday World & Splashin' Safari for their support and memories, including Leah Koch; Matt Blumhardt; Mike Johannes, retired director of sales; Tony Perkins, director of maintenance; and Sean Strahl, maintenance planner. He is also grateful to several employees of The Gravity Group including Lawrence "Larry" Bill, engineer and principal; Michael Graham, engineer and principal; Korey Kiepert, engineer and principal; and Chad Miller, engineer and principal; along with Dennis McNulty, former engineer for Custom Coasters International; and Tim O'Brien, former editor, *Amusement Business*, retired. He is especially appreciative of the assistance of his son David Hahner III in researching and editing his portion of the book.

Nell Hedge would like to thank the thousands of guests who visit the Santa Claus Museum & Village and who share their memories and help keep the spirit of Christmas alive! Thanks also to Mrs. Koch and her passion for history and love of Spencer County and to my family for taking me on the best ride of my life!

And Leah Koch would like to thank the people that made the most difficult years a little easier: Matt Eckert, Chip Cleary, Terry Farmer, Mike Wiederkehr, and most importantly, Mom. Thank you for fighting for us.

Introduction

Growing up, the highlight of every summer for me was getting to go to Santa Claus Land (and later Holiday World) for a day of absolute fun. I could not wait to ride the Antique Cars, Paul Revere's Midnight Ride, the Firecracker, the Freedom Train . . . the list was endless. It was a day that I got to spend with my family with no other purpose than to have the best day ever, and in the process, create memories that have lasted a lifetime.

Fast-forward to my college years and the park had added Splashin' Safari and would build The Raven. I had several good friends who worked here as seasonal team members, and they absolutely loved it. I personally loved to bring friends to show off this amazing place right in "my backyard."

It was my home park.

Fast-forward to after college and I was a senior auditor for a large public accounting firm. A friend of mine told me about an opening at the park for a director of accounting and finance. At the time, I was not interested. However, I did agree to come talk to the president of the park one weekend while I was home. I met with Will Koch, and that day my life changed forever.

Will and I had probably a three-hour interview that day. However, it did not feel like an interview at all. It felt like a good friend was passionately telling me about what he does and why he does it. Will called me the next day and offered me the job and told me that he could not see anyone else in the role, that I was a perfect fit for the company. I took the job and the rest is history.

Through the years, Will became one of my very best friends and mentors. In 2007, he promoted me to general manager. Tragically, Will passed in 2010. This not only had a monumental effect on his family and me but also on our company and team members and the entire industry. He truly was and is a legend. When his family asked me to assume the role of president and CEO after his passing, it was an overwhelming honor. To be able to follow in his footsteps and lead this incredible park and transition into the fourth generation is greater than I would have ever imagined. I now understand the passion Will had on that first day I met him. I have it too.

In my 21 years here, there have been countless highs and lows, a roller coaster ride, you might say. We have had tremendous growth, we have three world-class wooden coasters, we have the nation's first launched wing coaster, we are the Water Coaster Capital of the World, we have been voted the Cleanest and Friendliest Park numerous times, we won the Applause Award . . . the list goes on and on. We have also seen our share of downturns, most notably with the recent pandemic. However, even with this challenge, we excelled and rose above the adversity.

I am so excited for you to enjoy this book and learn about our rich history as we celebrate 75 years of creating memories that last a lifetime. As you do, I think you too will understand and appreciate the passion we have. You will see why it was my "home park." It is and forever will be.

Matt Eckert, president and CEO of
Holiday World & Splashin' Safari

A Town Called Santa Claus

Nell Hedge

Many a curious traveler has taken a detour while on I-64 in southern Indiana. The name "Santa Claus" posted at exit 63 is just too much for true Christmas-loving folks to pass up, and many are surprised by the attractions and history of this small community.

Just seven and a half miles from the exit, past the curve along State Road 245, today's travelers come across a small park. It is not just any park with picnic pavilions and playground equipment but instead contains features not seen anywhere else. Named the Santa Claus Museum & Village, the park contains a church dating back to 1880 and a small building that once served as a post office. They were both moved here from elsewhere in the community to accompany a large statue of Santa Claus. The final building in the complex contains a museum that not only weaves these seemingly disconnected structures together but tells the story about the role each one played in the creation of the nation's first theme park.

The Beginning of a Community

Southern Indiana and Spencer County were settled by hearty Germanic, English, and Scots-Irish peoples that were yeoman farmers who raised their own livestock and farmed their own land. Indiana achieved statehood in 1816, and by 1818, Spencer County was settled along the Ohio River in nine townships.

One of those early settler families arrived in 1816 when the Lincolns—Thomas, Nancy, and their two children: nine-year-old Sarah and seven-year-old Abraham—packed up and left Kentucky for the new frontier in southern Indiana. The Lincolns had a 160-acre claim in the unsettled wilderness. Long before he entertained thoughts of becoming president, young Abraham became skilled with an axe and plow and was expected to help out around the farm. Despite having little free time, he discovered the joy of reading and became a voracious reader. With educational opportunities lacking, he became his own teacher.

In 1828, at the age of 19, Abraham was hired to help deliver a flatboat to New Orleans. It was after seeing and learning about the world while on his trip that he became interested in politics. At the urging of relatives, the Lincoln family decided to move to Illinois in 1830.

Facing, The original Santa Claus post office, constructed in 1856, has since been relocated to the Santa Claus Museum and serves as the hub of the community's letter-writing operation. *Jim Futrell photo.*

Chronology

1846
Town of Santa Fee laid out in southern Indiana

Mid-1850s
After the original town name was turned down by the Postal Service, a town meeting was held, supposedly on Christmas Eve, where Santa Claus was chosen as the town's new name

May 21, 1856
The community's name was officially recognized as Santa Claus by the US Postal Service. The town's original post office opened soon after

1873
George Koch, who left Germany for the United States in 1843, arrived in Evansville, Indiana, and established the George Koch Tin Shop

June 12, 1882
Santa Claus Land founder Louis J. Koch is born

1903
George Koch's son Louis married Clarice, and they had nine children. Fifth child William (Bill) was born in 1915

1914
Santa Claus Postmaster James Martin began mailing response letters from Santa to children who mailed Christmas lists to Santa Claus, Indiana

1916
Raymond Joseph "Jim" Yellig portrayed Santa for the first time at the Brooklyn Shipyard. When he returned to Santa Claus, he began playing the role in town and helping his friend James Martin answer letters

1930
Robert Ripley features Santa Claus and its letter campaign in his Ripley's *Believe it or Not* feature, increasing the volume of mail

December 22, 1935
Santa Claus Park unveils 22-foot-tall, 40-ton statue of Santa Claus. Nearby, the Candy Castle opens

Late 1930s
Louis J. Koch begins purchasing land in Santa Claus with the intent of developing a Christmas attraction

1940
The town was electrified and its road were paved for the first time

August 4, 1945
Louis J. Koch begins construction on Santa Claus Land

Santa Claus's second post office was where the town's famous letter-writing operation began in 1914. *Holiday World photo.*

Becoming Santa Claus

In 1846, a small farming community, later known as Santa Fee, was laid out just five miles to the east of the Lincoln homestead. By the mid-1850s, it was prospering and was home to more than 40 families. The town initially applied for a post office under the name of Santa Fee, Indiana, but the Post Office Department withheld approval and instructed the town to choose a new name. There was already a post office in a town named Santa Fe, Indiana, and despite the different spelling, the two names were just too similar.

According to legend, the townsfolk were gathered in a small log church on Christmas Eve discussing a new name for the town. Suddenly, a gust of wind blew open the door and the sound of sleigh bells drifted into the cozy room. There was no sleigh in sight, but the children yelled, "It's Santa Claus!" and the town

leaders decided that Santa Claus would be a fine name for their little settlement. While the exact details of how the town of Santa Claus was named may never be known, there is no doubt that the town name was officially approved by the Post Office Department in 1856. A new post office building soon followed in the village.

That tiny building still exists today at the Santa Claus Museum. In 1946, its days as a post office long past, it was relocated from the community to the then-new Santa Claus Land. In its new location, the building served as the park's House of Dolls attraction for 65 years before it was moved to the museum in 2012. In its new role, it serves as the hub of the community's Christmas letter-writing operation.

By the early twentieth century, the community had outgrown the original post office. A new post office was erected in Santa Claus, Indiana, and with that, the town was truly put on the map. Given the town's unique name, letters began arriving addressed to Santa Claus.

In 1914, James Martin, took over the duties as the town postmaster from his father. He had noticed the letters addressed to Santa Claus drifting into the post office during the Christmas season from children around the country mailing their requests. Martin didn't think the children's letters should go unanswered, and at his own expense, he began sending replies. He took it upon himself to be the postal hub for Santa Claus and in 1927 worked to get the town's name restored to the two-word "Santa Claus," reversing an 1895 directive by the Post Office giving the town a one-word name—"Santaclaus"—as part of an effort to standardize community names throughout the country.

By now, post offices around the country were forwarding letters to Santa to the Santa Claus post office, and in 1930, Robert Ripley featured the town and its growing letter-writing operation in his *Believe*

With the increasing flood of Christmas letters into Santa Claus, members of the town's American Legion Post stepped up to help answer them. *Santa Claus Museum photo.*

it or Not cartoon. One year later, the Santa Claus post office received, and James Martin hand-canceled, a huge postcard more than four feet wide. A newspaper in Indianapolis reported that it was the largest postcard ever mailed in the world. The publicity from *Believe it or Not* and the giant postcard resulted in a huge increase of mail that Christmas—so much so that the United States postmaster suggested the community change its name to stop the blizzard of Christmas mail. But community outcry, led by

James Martin, extended up to the federal level and succeeded in stopping the change.

Instead, Martin rallied the community to expand the effort and recruited his friend, Jim Yellig to help him. Yellig had retired from a long naval career and returned to his home in southern Indiana to open a restaurant. He became the first commander of the newly formed American Legion Post in Santa Claus. Yellig enlisted the post in the Christmas letter effort and organized groups of helpers from the local typing

Santa Jim took over the letter-writing operation following the passing of James Martin and made it part of the town's culture. *Santa Claus Museum photo.*

Santa Jim Yellig married Isabelle Schue in 1924, and she served as his faithful Mrs. Santa for 60 years. *Holiday World photo.*

classes at the high school, students at the Archabbey in Saint Meinrad, and the Sisters of Saint Benedict in Ferdinand, Indiana.

Martin passed away in 1935, but a Santa Claus postmark remains a cherished holiday greeting for many people. In recent years, the Santa Claus post office handles more than 400,000 pieces of mail in December compared to 13,000 in a normal month. To this day, its Santa Claus's letter operation remains a family affair with Jim Yellig's daughter Pat Koch leading the community effort.

The Santa of Santa Claus

There couldn't have been a better person than Yellig to keep the tradition alive, for he was Santa Claus. Jim's name wasn't actually Jim after all. He was born Raymond Joseph Yellig and was the baby boy with two older sisters. They loved to tote him around and referred to him as their "Little Jimmy" and the name stuck.

His lifelong devotion to the spirit of Santa Claus began when he was a young sailor serving on the USS

New York. In 1914, he played Santa Claus for the first time for underprivileged children in Brooklyn, and the feeling he received by bringing joy to the children never left him. During World War I, he prayed, "If you get me through this war, Lord, I will forever be Santa Claus."

Yellig married Isabelle Schue in 1924 and they had two children—Raymond, who also had a long navy career and Patricia (now Pat Koch), who had a much different calling. Jim was very proud of his roots and spoke happily of his home in Mariah Hill, Indiana, and the nearby town of Santa Claus.

Following his service, Jim returned home and began serving as Santa Claus in the community. Jim was Santa year-round. He participated in hundreds of parades and events as Santa Claus, often for the American Legion. Pat Koch remembers a trip to Miami for the American Legion Christmas Parade. "There was a rumor that Santa had traveled to Florida with his "reindeer" on the train. People became worried that the animals were getting too hot . . . all while Jim was delighting in his secret. The reindeer were actually papier mâché. He got a great laugh and lots of publicity for it!"

Jim made numerous appearances in Santa Claus during the 1930s and 1940s, so when Santa Claus Land opened in 1946, there was no question who would be Santa at the new attraction. Santa Jim held court in the toy shop at Santa Claus Land. There was a magical painted mural with a sleigh, elves, and a wintery scene as the backdrop to Santa Jim's chair. Thousands of children sat on his lap and whispered their Christmas wishes. Visitors often comment with happy memories of getting their family Christmas picture taken on Santa Jim's lap in front of the mural. The mural is now on display at the Santa Claus Museum.

Santa Jim's grandchildren remember being at their grandparents' house on Christmas Eve and their grandfather receiving calls from children and families putting in last-minute wishes and wondering when he would be at their house. Jim believed that there was a right way and wrong way to be Santa. He published a booklet to help train Santas: *It's Fun to a be a Real Santa Claus*. Many current-day Santas model their Santa suits, beards, glasses, and belt from the example of Santa Jim Yellig. He holds a special place in the history of Santa Claus and Santa Claus Land. Santa Jim was considered such an influential Santa Claus that he was a charter member of the International Santa Claus Hall of Fame.

Jim Yellig continued to play the role at Santa Claus Land until he passed away in 1984 at the age of 90. By then it was estimated that one million children had sat on his knee.

A Match Made in Santa Claus

The marriage of Santa's daughter and the son of the founder of Santa Claus Land sounds like a Christmas wish come true. Bill Koch, the fifth child of Santa Claus Land founder Louis J. Koch, started working at the family's industrial business, George Koch Sons, in 1938 after he graduated from Purdue University. He served in the US Navy during World War II, and following the war he accepted a position at Santa Claus Land, a subsidiary of George Koch Sons. While Bill Koch was working on plans to expand and build Santa Claus Land, Pat Yellig, Santa Jim's daughter, went to nursing school and was a sister in the Daughters of Charity nursing order. Pat lived in St. Louis until 1960 when she was called home to help care for her ailing dad.

Bill Koch had become a close family friend of the Yelligs, and it was a snowy night when Pat was set to arrive at the train station in Washington, Indiana, and her parents asked Bill to pick her up. Bill had become a fixture in and around Santa Claus and was acquainted with many people Pat knew and grew up with. After attending a birthday party together and spending time with her family, Pat decided she still had work to do as a nurse and moved back to St. Louis. Bill visited many times, telling Pat he was there on business, but he was really just coming to see her. After a few months, Bill asked her to come home and marry him. Fittingly, the wedding was in December 1960.

Bill and Pat were 17 years apart in age, but Pat said, "The age difference was never an issue—it just worked!" Bill and Pat had five children between 1961 and 1967. Bill had a dream and plan for the town of Santa Claus and the future of Santa Claus Land. Bill and Pat had a great business working relationship; Bill liked to work with numbers away from the spotlight and Pat became the face of the park. Santa Claus Land was a family venture where everyone pitched in and helped in some way almost as soon as they could walk! Natalie, the youngest of the siblings, remembers helping with cotton candy and drinks before she knew how to make change. The Koch kids all worked at the park and were paid just like everyone else. Every Sunday, the family ate together at the Christmas Room for lunch, and the kids had swimming lessons at Christmas Lake beach. Family vacations were centered around visiting other amusement parks to see what they liked and could add to Santa Claus Land. Vacations also included board meetings where Bill would discuss the future of the park with the family. The Koch kids all learned about *Robert's Rules of Order*, making motions, quarterly financials, and the business side of the park as well as entertainment.

Pat Koch, who prefers to be called Mrs. Koch, is still active in all things Santa Claus, Indiana, at 90 years old. Mrs. Koch is very proud of her Spencer County roots and works really hard to make sure the history of the town is not forgotten. She helped establish the Santa Claus Museum & Village in 2012

Santa Claus Land founder Louis J. Koch thought a town named Santa Claus needed need an attraction for children visiting the community. *Holiday World photo.*

and works tirelessly during the holiday season to make sure that each and every letter sent to Santa Claus gets a personal response.

Bill and Pat instilled their love for community and strong work ethic to their children. All of the children attended Heritage Hills High School and went on to earn degrees from higher education institutions. Will, Dan, and Natalie all held leadership roles at Holiday World and Splashin' Safari, while Kristi and Philip were local businesses owners. The fourth generation of Koch kids are now carrying the torch for the future.

Making Santa Claus a Destination

When a community chooses a name like Santa Claus, it starts to attract curiosity seekers, and it's only a matter of time until someone opens an attraction to take advantage of the traffic. As Santa Claus's reputation grew in the early 1930s, it caught the attention of two entrepreneurs, Milton Harris and Carl Barrett. But after all was said and done, the two men would have been on Santa's Naughty List. Land was leased and sold, and a legal battle for control over the land hit the courts. Unresolved, the dispute later helped clear the way for Louis J. Koch to begin purchasing land in the late 1930s that he used to build Santa Claus Land.

Milton Harris gave up his law practice in Vincennes, Indiana, and initially planned to manufacture decorative sleighs in Santa Claus. He worked closely with Postmaster James Martin and set about establishing a town newspaper and a chamber of commerce. But soon Harris started making plans for something grander—Santa Claus Town.

Harris was able to get the backing of the Curtiss Candy Company and began leasing land in the area, eventually amassing more than a thousand acres. He started construction on the first feature—the Candy Castle—in 1932, selecting the castle design because Santa was thought to live in one. He also started making plans to develop an Enchanted Forest and Toyland Workshops for manufacturing and mailing of toys with the "Santa Claus" postmark. The Candy Castle was dedicated on Sunday, December 22, 1935, before a huge crowd, and Santa Jim was a featured speaker.

Santa Claus Town expanded in 1936 with the addition of Santa's Workshop and the Toy Village. In Santa's Workshop, children could experience the magic of watching Santa Claus make toys in a fully functional wood shop. The Toy Village featured eight miniature fairy-tale buildings sponsored by America's leading toy manufacturers including Daisy (air rifles), Lionel (electric trains), Buddy L (steel trucks), Wyandotte (pop guns), and Strombecker (doll furniture). No admission was charged to enter these buildings, and nothing was for sale. Children could simply play and have fun with all the popular toys of the day. As America struggled through the Great Depression and many families did without, the Toy Village offered thousands of children the Christmas morning they otherwise wouldn't have had.

Around the same time, another businessman from Chicago, Carl Barrett, also had his eyes set on the potential of the famously named Santa Claus, Indiana. Barrett helped fund his dreams of development with the establishment of the Santa Claus Good Fellowship Club. The club was centered on the idea of perpetuating the spirit of Christmas and building Santa Claus Park. Milton Harris already held the lease on the land that Barrett purchased for the park site. Barrett went ahead with his plans while Harris filed a lawsuit. The main attraction of the park would be a giant Santa Claus statue. Construction of the statue began in the summer of 1935. The 22-foot-tall statue was made of forty tons of concrete with a granite-like finish. The base of the statue reads, "Dedicated to the children of the world in memory of undying love." It was surrounded by a 20-foot-wide Christmas star and faced east toward biblical Bethlehem. Carl Barrett also chose December 22, 1935, as the day to unveil his Santa statue. It is noted that more than one thousand people attended the ceremonies that day in Santa Claus. The statue was officially dedicated on Christmas Day, 1935.

Unfortunately, the legal battles between Harris and Barrett halted their plans. Most development was stopped while the Indiana Supreme Court reviewed the case. The court ruled that Harris' lease was valid with no damages paid and Barrett's Santa statue was allowed to remain. But the world was about to face much more serious worries.

With the United States joining World War II in 1941, all dreams and plans for Santa Claus were deferred as tourism stopped due to limited gasoline supplies and the rationing of tires. Santa Claus Town became a shadow of what it once was.

After the war, Santa Claus Town creator Milton Harris began working to try to return the attraction to its original glory. Sadly, however, Harris passed away unexpectedly in 1950, and his dream was never fully realized. His attraction was abandoned while Barnett's Santa Claus Park fell into a state of neglect.

While the dreams of Harris and Barrett were but brief flickers in the history of the town, their legacies remain. The Candy Castle was purchased by a local business owner in 2005 and reopened in 2006. Unfortunately, Santa's Workshop and the Toy Village remain abandoned and in ruins to this day. Meanwhile, the former grounds of Barrett's Santa Claus Park were acquired for the new home of Santa Claus Museum & Village, and the neglected statue was restored in 2011.

By the 1930s, the post office was called the Santa Claus headquarters. In 1947, the post office moved to Santa Claus Land, and eventually the building was demolished in 1964. *Jim Futrell collection.*

How It Came To Be

But the story of the Koch family and their arrival in Santa Claus goes back to 1843 when George Koch left Germany for the United States. He arrived in Evansville, Indiana, in 1873 and established the George Koch Tin Shop with financial help from his family. After George's death in 1903, his widow Mary and her three sons changed the name of the company to George Koch Sons, Incorporated. All became directors and officers in the company, and son Louis was named secretary and treasurer. Louis married Clarice in 1903 and had nine children with William (Bill) as their middle fifth child.

The connection to Santa and Christmas as a lifetime endeavor began for the Koch family with Louis and Clarice and their children in 1914. During World War I, no toys were imported from Europe and Louis experimented and developed tin horns as Christmas gifts for his children. Orders came pouring in and George Koch Sons began production of its first mass-produced manufactured product.

The Candy Castle was opened by Milton Harris in 1935 as the first phase in a planned tourist attraction that was sidetracked by World War II. *Santa Claus Museum photo.*

Between the world wars, Louis and Clarice dreamed, conceived, and planned the idea of a children's park in the hills of southern Indiana, and they felt with the town named Santa Claus, there should be more for children to do. This was said to be a "retirement project" for Louis.

Louis J. Koch would think of the thousands of tourists who would arrive in Santa Claus on a family drive during the Christmas season and find little to do other than visit the post office. Even with the magical town name, Santa Claus at that time was still a small farming community without electricity or paved roads.

Past attempts to develop a tourist attraction for visitors had failed. In 1935, Milton Harris, started to develop Santa Claus Town by opening the Candy Castle. Around the same time, another businessman from Chicago, Carl Barrett, established the Santa Claus Good Fellowship Club and began developing Santa Claus Park with its 22-foot-tall

Above, A young Pat and Ray Yellig visit the Santa Claus statue that was erected in Santa Claus Park in 1935. *Santa Claus Museum photo.*

Children could visit the wishing well at Santa Claus Park. *Santa Claus Museum photo.*

statue of Santa Claus. Unfortunately, the competing concepts devolved into lawsuits filed between the two businessmen, and with the advent of World War II and the halt of pleasure travel, they became neglected.

World War II deferred Louis J. Koch's dreams too but did not kill them. Before the war, Louis J. Koch started to lay the groundwork to realize his dream and began purchasing property that was once leased by Milton Harris. He built a small residence on site and was very involved in overseeing construction after they broke ground on August 4, 1945. Louis J. Koch's Santa Claus Land opened a year later, and Santa Claus and the amusement park industry would never be the same.

A Theme Park Comes to Santa Claus

1946–1969

Jim Futrell

The United States of the late 1940s was a rapidly changing place. With World War II and the dark days of the Great Depression in the rearview mirror, a renewed sense of optimism and growing prosperity spread throughout the nation. Returning servicemen were anxious to resume their civilian lives and realize their share of the American dream by moving to the suburbs and starting families. And these growing families had an increasing appetite for entertainment.

This renewed sense of optimism also spread to the amusement park industry. At the time, the industry was dominated by large, family-owned amusement parks located in urban centers. With the financial and materials limitations of the 1930s and 1940s behind them, these facilities launched major expansion and modernization programs. Surrounding Santa Claus, amusement parks such as Indianapolis's Riverside Amusement Park, Louisville's Fontainne Ferry, Cincinnati's Coney Island, and Forest Park Highlands in St. Louis all upgraded their facilities and added new rides. The latter three all built huge new roller coasters, making a loud statement about the optimism they felt for the postwar world.

Other new amusement parks began opening, many of which catered to growing suburban families. Called "kiddielands," they were simple roadside attractions located near new shopping malls and featuring scaled-down rides for small children.

This environment provided the perfect opportunity for Louis J. Koch to realize his longtime dream. On the 260 acres of farmland he purchased nearly a decade earlier, Koch began building a place to provide amusement and entertainment to the thousands of children who visited the town annually to take in the spirit of Santa Claus. Koch took a different approach than the other amusement parks of the time as the entire attraction was devoted to a celebration of Christmas, which seemed only natural in a town called Santa Claus.

There were other themed attractions operating in the country—most notably Knott's Berry Farm in California. Knott's got its start in 1920 when Walter Knott started farming berries. In 1934, his wife Cordelia started serving their famous chicken dinners, and in 1940, Knott started building his Ghost Town to entertain people waiting for their turn to eat. But Louis J. Koch's "children's paradise" was different, as it represented the first time an amusement park had been built from the ground up revolving around a singular theme with a selection of attractions supporting that story—the first theme park.

Chronology

August 3, 1946
Santa Claus Land first opens for visitors. A grand opening is held on September 1

1947
Santa Claus Land Railroad, the House of Dolls, the Nativity, and the Jeep-Go-Round open

1948
Deer Farm opens

1950
The Miniature Circus is added

1953
Hall of Famous Americans Wax Museum Opens

1955
Admission charged for the first time

1957
Santa Claus Land undergoes a major expansion, adding Pioneerland, Pleasureland, the Dogwood Amphitheater, and Lake Rudolph

1958
The German Band begins performances in the park and becomes a fixture for the next twenty years

1959
Willie Bartley's *Water Ski Thrill Show* begins three-season run on Lake Rudolph

1963
Santa Claus Land opens its campground

1965
Several new attractions debut including the Seahorse ride, the Transportation Museum, and the Riverboat Museum

1966
Development begins on Christmas Lake Village

View of Santa Claus Statue and Main Lodge, Santa Claus Land
Santa Claus, Indiana

Fronting Highway 162, the Main Lodge was the heart of Santa Claus Land when it opened. *Jim Futrell collection.*

Construction began on the Kochs' new park in August 1945 and almost exactly a year later, on August 3, 1946, guests first started being admitted to the facility, which was still under construction. "Santa Claus Land, long a cherished dream that has brought joy to the hearts of children everywhere will soon become reality," the Princeton, Indiana, *Daily Clarion* proclaimed before the official grand opening on September 1, 1946.

The new 40-acre attraction fronted Indiana Route 162. The heart of the park was the Main Lodge. Designed to resemble an Alpine village, the building was a series of interconnected units. The first was a restaurant, known for its chicken dinners, which included a special children's soda fountain with scaled-down tables and chairs. Next came the toy and gift shop and then the exhibit hall with its Toyland exhibit. Toyland contained 76 glass-fronted booths displaying toys from around the world and throughout history. Initially Koch had trouble getting foreign toys to display as much of the world was still recovering from the war.

Toyland also contained displays of the newest toys from leading manufacturers. For many years, Koch would place advertisements in toy industry publications, soliciting manufacturers to display their latest products at Santa Claus Land. Of course, this was where children could visit with Santa and point out which toys they would like him to bring them for Christmas. Rounding out the features in the Main Lodge was a souvenir shop.

Adorning the front of the building was a larger-than-life statue of Santa Claus, billed as the first and only full-color statue of Santa in the world.

Above, Jim Yellig was Santa Claus Land's original Santa, a role he played for the next 38 years. *Holiday World photo*.

Top right, Despite all of the other attractions, a visit with Santa was the main reason to visit Santa Claus Land. *Holiday World photo*.

Right, Until the late 1950s, this statue greeted guests as they arrived at Santa Claus Land. *Jim Futrell collection*.

In a wooded area located between the highway and the Main Lodge, guests could explore the Enchanted Trail, a one-third-mile path that took guests past sculptured Mother Goose characters like Little Boy Blue; Wynken, Blynken and Nod; Humpty Dumpty; Jack and Jill; Jack and the Beanstalk; and Little Miss Muffet.

Little Miss Muffet was one of the many storybook tales recreated on the Enchanted Trail. *Jim Futrell collection.*

The kiddie train was the first ride to open at Santa Claus Land. *Jim Futrell collection.*

Young visitors enjoying Little Boy Blue on the Enchanted Trail. *Jim Futrell collection.*

Louis J. Koch loved trains so much that he had one in the backyard of his Evansville home. So, it's not surprising that the park's initial rides would be trains.

The first one to open was a kiddie train that traveled in an oval in front of the Main Lodge. It was available for Santa Claus Land's smallest guests and stood just 18 inches high and 15 feet long. Initially rides were free, but soon tickets were five cents each. Louis's son Bill later admitted to the New York *Daily News* that he had to charge admission because "those kids really fought one another to get on when we were running it for free."

But it was the other train that ended up being one of the park's most enduring and best loved attractions.

The Santa Claus Land Railroad was Santa Claus Land's most enduring attraction, operating 65 years. *Jim Futrell collection.*

Louis J. Koch hired Ted Buehn, a model train enthusiast, to build a ⅛-scale train based on a Baltimore & Ohio steam locomotive that was constructed at the family's Evansville business, George Koch Sons. The train, initially located in a separate section of the park with its own parking area, measured 4 feet high and 59 feet long and featured two coaches—an enclosed car exclusively for the use of small children and one for their parents. It traveled on a half-mile-long track taking riders on a "Trip Around the World" through a tunnel, over a bridge, and past a miniature Atlantic Ocean and replicas of the Grand Canyon, the Swiss Alps, and the Pyramids.

While the train faithfully chugged along its circular path for the next 65 years, its identity changed over time, becoming the Fairyland Railroad in the 1950s and, following the relocation of the Mother Goose figure to the train route around 1960, the Mother Goose Land Train.

A Growing Business

Santa Claus Land entered 1947 continuing to grow. Koch relocated the original Santa Claus Post Office to the property, between the Main Lodge and the Santa Claus Land Railroad. Built in 1856 as a general store, the simple building was restored and transformed into the House of Dolls, containing more than one thousand antique dolls. Inspired by the collection of Louis J. Koch's daughter, Helen, the House of Dolls eventually grew to feature more than two thousand dolls including miniatures of historical characters: presidents, inventors, clergy members, and artists. When the exhibit was closed in 2011, the building was moved to nearby Santa Claus Museum and Village, where it remains an important part of community history and the heart of the town's Christmas letter operation.

Joining the kiddie train was the Jeep-Go-Round. The first ride of its type, the miniature jeeps traveled

Above, Santa Claus Land moved the original Santa Claus post office to the property and used it as the House of Dolls. *Jim Futrell collection.*

Left, More than 1,000 dolls were on display when House of Dolls opened in 1947. *Holiday World photo.*

in a circular path, while kids could turn the steering wheel, work the turn signal and step on the brake pedal.

Nearby, the true meaning of Christmas was recognized with the opening of the Nativity scene, an 18-foot-long, 5-foot-tall diorama described by newspapers as "expertly detailed and artistically prepared." It featured nine life-sized concrete figures sculpted by Lewis Sorensen, painted in a style of clothing common at the time.

Sorensen was a well-known doll designer. Originally from Utah, he began working at an early age in fashion design, eventually becoming a leading designer of dolls. In fact, after World War II, Eleanor Roosevelt commissioned Mr. Sorensen to create a set

Above, The Jeep-Go-Round was the first ride of its kind when it opened at Santa Claus Land in 1947. *Holiday World photo.*

Right, Well-known doll designer Lewis Sorensen was hired to create Santa Claus Land's life-sized Nativity in 1947. *Jim Futrell collection.*

of presidential dolls for her home in Hyde Park, New York.

The figures were placed in a building constructed of hand-hewn fieldstone taken from the basement of the original Santa Claus post office when it was relocated to the park. The upper half of the structure was made of hand-hewn oak logs taken from a 100-year-old area home.

Rounding out the additions was a two-story building near the Main Lodge that contained a new expanded toy shop on the first floor and a warehouse upstairs. Visitors could select toys at the shop and have them shipped directly from Santa Claus with the world-famous postmark. For many years, Santa Claus Land also curated a selection of fifty special toys that department stores could promote through a separate catalog. Customers could order the toys and the department store would have them shipped directly from Santa Claus Land.

On October 5, 1947, Santa Claus Land's efforts to move the town post office to the park came to fruition. A new 1,500-square-foot modern post office took up residence in the Main Lodge, between the gift shop and toy museum.

Lewis Sorensen had a long relationship with Santa Claus Land, creating many of the figures for the exhibits and painting the murals in the Christmas Room. *Holiday World photo.*

In October 1947, Santa Claus Land succeeded in getting the town post office moved to the park. *Holiday World photo.*

Renovations and expansions continued during Santa Claus Land's third season as the Deer Farm debuted. Located in the woods behind the Main Lodge, the farm started with a family of eight deer named after Santa's herd and later grew to fourteen European white fallow deer and several peacocks. It was soon expanded to include "Animals of Christmas, Farm and Mother Goose Legend" according to brochures from the era.

In addition, the park's restaurant was transformed into the Christmas Room, featuring scaled-down tables and chairs for children, distinctive murals, and bowls of tropical fish adorning the room. Lewis Sorenson was brought back to adorn the walls in hand-painted Christmas murals. For years, a baked Alaska dessert was a beloved tradition at the Christmas Room.

The increasingly popular park reported a 26 percent increase in business and, thanks to mild weather, on Sunday, December 11, 1948, 25,000 cars visited the town of Santa Claus, with many stopping off at Santa Claus Land.

Above, Added in 1948, Santa Claus Land's Deer Farm was a fixture for nearly 30 years. *Jim Futrell collection.*

Right, Christmas dinners at the Christmas Room restaurant were a beloved tradition for many years. *Holiday World photo.*

Unlike today, the Christmas season was when visitation peaked at Santa Claus Land in the early years. *Holiday World photo.*

But probably the most significant development for the future of Santa Claus Land was the change in management. Initially, responsibility for operating the fledgling operation was split among the numerous members of the Koch family. But in 1948, Bill Koch, Louis and Clarice Koch's fifth child, began operating the park full time. Initially, he was hesitant about joining the operation, but he also saw the potential for Santa Claus Land in the postwar amusement park industry. In the end it was a great decision, as Bill would soon prove himself quite adept at reading the market and guiding Santa Claus Land to ever greater heights.

With the dawn of the 1950s, the Miniature Circus joined the lineup at Santa Claus Land. Located in a new building behind the Main Lodge, visitors could enjoy miniature recreations of a complete circus including sideshows, concessions, menagerie, the three-ring big top, the backyard, and even a full-scale

Abraham Lincoln, who spent his childhood near Santa Claus, was one of the dozens of figures displayed in the Hall of Famous Americans. *Holiday World photo.*

Top, The Miniature Circus was given its own building when it opened in 1950. *Jim Futrell collection.*

Above, Opened in 1953, the Hall of Famous Americans wax museum was a fixture for the next 50 seasons. *Holiday World photo.*

circus parade. Santa Claus Land purchased the circus from Mr. and Mrs. W. S. Colvin of Oklahoma, who spent six years as a family carving the thousands of figures by hand.

By now, Santa Claus Land was a well-established destination with total attendance estimated at 250,000. The park was proud of the fact that, despite popular perception, two-thirds of the visitors were adults. On Sunday, December 2, 1951, attendance totaled 23,000 people from 14 states, a record broken four days later for a special event commemorating the tenth anniversary of Pearl Harbor.

While Santa Claus Land had undoubtedly become a success, the demands of running the growing operation, along with increased business from the Department of Defense at the company's Evansville metals plant was starting to take a toll on Louis J. Koch's health. Koch and his nine children voted to place the park up for sale, a decision opposed by the park's employees.

Above, By the early 1950s, Santa Claus Land's kiddieland had grown to three rides with the addition of the kiddie boat ride. *Holiday World photo.*

Left, The circus contained thousands of miniature figures hand-carved by the Colvin family of Oklahoma. *Jim Futrell collection.*

Birth of a Genre

When the theme park industry first began, it was common for entrepreneurs to adapt a single theme using a concept that was well known to the general public and easily adaptable without violating any copyright laws. As a result, most of these early theme parks revolved around three main concepts—the "Wild West," fairy tales, or Christmas—and by the 1960s, there were dozens of these parks spread throughout the country.

Knott's Berry Farm's Ghost Town is widely known as the pioneer of the Wild West theme park. But it was a little different in that Walter Knott relocated authentic buildings from ghost towns throughout the West to his already-thriving berry farm and restaurant. Meanwhile, the first Wild West theme park developed from the ground up using recreations of building from the era is thought to be Frontier Town of the Adirondacks, North Hudson, New York, which operated from 1952 until 1999.

New York's Adirondack region was something of an incubator of the early theme park industry and was the home of Arto Monaco, who designed many of them throughout the region. He opened his own park, Land of Make Believe, in 1954. and it emphasized attractions that kids actively participated in. It remained popular until it closed in 1979.

But Monaco also worked with theme park pioneer Charles Wood to design Storytown USA in Lake George. When it opened in 1954, it was thought to be the first theme park that utilized fairy-tale characters as its central identity. It is now known as The Great Escape and is part of the Six Flags chain.

While Santa Claus Land was the undisputed originator of the Christmas park genre, it was only a matter of time before others embraced the theme. In 1949, Julian Reiss, inspired by a story he told his daughter, hired Monaco to recreate Santa's North Pole village in the Adirondack Mountains. Known as Santa's Workshop, the park remains in operation.

California developer Glenn Holland saw a *Saturday Evening Post* story about the New York project and set up a publicly traded corporation to develop a chain of Santa's Villages throughout the country, inspired by conversations with his friends Dick and Mac McDonald, of restaurant fame.

He opened his first Santa's Village on Memorial Day in 1955, in Skyforest, California, followed by a second in 1957 near Scotts Valley in Northern California. The third Santa's Village opened in 1959 in the Chicago suburb of East Dundee. It was the first theme park chain, predating the development of Six Flags by several years. Additional parks were planned in Richmond, Virginia, and Cherry Hill, New Jersey, but the company began experiencing financial problems due to the limited operating season of the Illinois location, and the parks were sold in 1965. The Scotts Valley park closed in 1979, while the other two experienced financial problems and closed for a time but are both are operating again under slightly different formats.

Overall, approximately a dozen Christmas theme parks in addition to Santa Claus Land opened throughout North America, and in a testament to their enduring appeal, seven remain in operation in Colorado, Illinois, New Hampshire, New York, North Carolina, and Vermont, each continuing to embrace a theme created by Louis J. Koch's Santa Claus Land.

"Dad started this as a hobby with the idea of having something children would enjoy. He's seventy years old now, and still works in an advisory capacity at our Evansville factory nearly every day. The plant's busy, but he insisted on driving up here frequently," Bill Koch told INS news service in June 1952. "Then he worries for fear things don't go right if he is not here. It seemed to the rest of the family that dad's hobby was hurting his health. The family owns all the stock in Koch Enterprises, so they voted to sell Santa Claus Land. I was the only one who opposed it."

But the family was going to be very selective in who the park would be sold to with the sales offering including several provisions to prevent over-commercialization of the business, including prohibiting the sale of alcoholic beverages. "We are asking that the new owner operate Santa Claus Land as it is being operated now. We don't want it to become just a Coney Island or highly commercialized promotional stunt," Bill Koch told the Richmond, Indiana, *Palladium Item* in June 1952.

Despite the park being for sale, Louis J. Koch was not going to neglect the operation. On July 4, 1953, the Hall of Famous Americans, a wax museum, opened in a newly constructed building next to the Santa Claus Land Railroad.

In keeping with Santa Claus Land's family-oriented theme, the $35,000 exhibit made sure not to include horror or criminal figures that would frighten children but rather focus on moments in history. Included were thirty-nine life-sized figures in seventeen settings including Thomas Jefferson signing the Declaration of Independence, George Washington at Mount Vernon, and, since he grew up nearby, three figures of Abraham Lincoln at different stages of his life—age seven when he was growing up near Santa Claus, age twenty-one when he left Indiana for Illinois, and as president. Other figures included Lillian Russell, Babe Ruth, Mark Twain, and

Stephen Foster. Eventually the hall would feature more than fifty figures. For many years, the Hall was overseen by Helen Koch Robb, Louis' daughter.

The park again turned to Sorensen to create the wax figures. In recent years he had begun wax modeling as a vocation and developed techniques to create more lifelike figures. He took on several additional projects for the park. For nine months, he worked at his California studio, and then he went to Santa Claus, where he spent another three months setting up his creations. Sorensen would return annually to maintain the figures and create new ones, and in 1954, he upgraded the park's Mother Goose displays.

Through the 1953 season, the sale sign hung over the park. With an asking price of $360,000, the operation generated three prospects—a grocery store chain owner from Cleveland, two souvenir manufacturers from Miami, and a businessperson from Detroit. There was also speculation that the state of Indiana might acquire the property as state park grounds, or the local Santa Claus Chamber of Commerce might purchase it.

But in the end, none of the interested purchasers could meet the Koch's demands to maintain integrity of the facility, and rather than selling the park, the family moved forward with long-term plans for development.

A Changing Park in a Changing Industry

The timing was vital because across the country in California, Walt Disney, then a legendary filmmaker, was forever changing the trajectory of the amusement industry by taking the embryonic concept of the theme park to the next level.

Rather than focusing on a singular theme like Christmas, Disneyland created an entire world of

The Pioneerland Train took guests on a 1-mile tour through the woods past the Pioneer Village and Indian Village. *Holiday World photo.*

five different themed areas that immersed guests in unique experiences. People would regard amusement parks in a completely different light from then on.

Ironically, during Disneyland's opening year in 1955, Santa Claus Land was featured on the Mickey Mouse Club and Disneyland television shows. The segment, titled "The Story of Santa Claus Land," was shot at the park on a fall morning with the trees in their full autumn glory. Starring two local children, the segment follows the letters they wrote to Santa through the mail to Santa Claus, played by Santa/Jim Yellig.

A critical change at Santa Claus Land that year was a revised admissions policy. Originally, admission to the grounds and certain exhibits, including visiting Santa Claus, was free with individual charges for other attractions. But in 1955, visitors were charged fifty cents to enter the grounds, and charges for the Deer Farm, the Miniature Circus, and Santa's Toyland were reduced.

Children under twelve, however, were free, in keeping with the original vision of Louis J. Koch, who desired that no child should have to pay to

visit with Santa—since it was a park for children, they should be given special privileges. With the town post office now located in Santa Claus Land behind the admission gate, the charge caused some consternation among local residents, but there was also a free pedestrian gate that provided post office access.

Santa Claus Land also broke new ground by offering one of the industry's first season passes, offering unlimited visits to Santa Claus area residents for one dollar.

With Disneyland changing the industry, Bill Koch announced plans to expand the park's size by 50 percent for the 1957 season, intending to turn the facility into a year-round recreational resort. Inspired by the multithemed lands at Disneyland, the first phase included a half dozen new attractions. Koch mentioned that while Santa Claus Land would remain unchanged as one part of the park, other attractions would each have their own theme with no relation to the Christmas motif.

The largest new attraction was Pioneerland. Located in the wooded area behind the Deer Farm,

Pioneerland featured an Indian Village and Pioneer Village with life-size figures created by Lewis Sorensen of native Americans, homesteaders, and even a prospector panning for gold in the natural wilderness.

To transport guests along the mile-long trail to Pioneerland, Santa Claus Land offered two modes of transportation—the Pioneerland Train and the Pioneerland Express Stagecoach. The train was a jeep camouflaged as an old-time steam engine pulling a three-car train.

Meanwhile, the Stagecoach was an actual antique built in the late 1800s that was originally used to pick up passengers at the Southern Railroad depot in nearby Dale to transport passengers to Wahl's Hotel.

Next to the Miniature Circus, a new kiddie ride area was created where the kiddie train, Jeep-Go-Round, and a recently added kiddie boat ride were relocated and joined by a Streetcar and the Pump-Its. The Streetcar was built by a park employee, while the Pump-Its, a handcar ride, was built by Harold Chance who would later go on to found Chance Rides, one of the world's largest amusement ride manufacturers.

Other new features added included the Dogwood Amphitheater, which could seat up to 10,000 people; a picnic area; the seven-acre Lake Rudolph, featuring bass fishing; an enlarged seven-acre parking area; and a new entrance arch at the parking lot where admission was collected. Finally, with mail volume continuing to increase, a new free-standing castle-like post office was erected along Highway 162.

Overall, Santa Claus Land's developed acreage increased from twenty to sixty and Bill Koch felt that the facility needed a new name that would be less seasonal and more fitting for a year-round operation.

The park held a naming contest among area children in which the winner received a lifetime pass, an oil portrait of themselves made by Lewis Sorensen, and a one-day reign as king or queen at a music festival held June 9 in the new amphitheater.

Top, The Pioneerland Train traveled past Lake Rudolph on its way to the Pioneer and Indian Villages. *Jim Futrell collection.*

Middle, Santa Claus Land acquired an antique stagecoach to provide rides along the Pioneerland trail. *Jim Futrell collection.*

Above, Pleasureland was an expanded kiddie ride area added in 1957. *Holiday World photo.*

Growth in traffic prompted Santa Claus Land to add a new entrance on Highway 162 in 1957. *Jim Futrell collection.*

A new castle-like post office along Highway 162 rounded out the 1957 expansion. *Holiday World photo.*

By the end of the 1950s, Santa Claus land had grown significantly since its founding. *Holiday World photo.*

The 67-foot tall "World's Largest Living Christmas Tree" was a park landmark for decades. *Jim Futrell collection.*

The Willie Bartley Ski Show was a major attraction for three seasons on Lake Rudolph. *Holiday World photo.*

Santa Claus Land received two hundred entries and some children submitted up to thirty-two different names. "A lot of thought was given to a name and the children came up with some very interesting names," said Bill Koch at the time. "But for one reason or another, either by usage at some other park or rather difficult spelling or hidden meaning, we eliminated all of them but the one entered by the winner," adding that many entries were similar to Disneyland.

But in the end, ten-year-old Hilbert Shruh Jr. of Huntingburg, Indiana, emerged as the winner. He submitted the name Pleasure Park, which was changed slightly to Pleasureland by the judges to go along with the idea of having a "land" in the name of each of the park's major divisions. Santa Claus Land was going to be one unit of Pleasureland. But when all was said and done, the park remained Santa Claus Land, and the Pleasureland name was given only to the new kiddie ride area. However, the name change foreshadowed what was to come thirty years later.

The newly expanded Santa Claus Land opened on Easter Sunday with an Easter parade for children, which became an enduring tradition to celebrate opening day. Advertisements invited families to see the "New Greater Santa Claus Land—The Show Place of Indiana." By the end of the year entertainment industry trade publication *Billboard* profiled Santa Claus Land and called it a theme park with "one of the earliest origins and one of the most ideal inspirations." It is one of the first documented instances of a media outlet using the term "theme park."

It was around this time that another long-time landmark made its debut when a 67-foot-tall cedar tree located on a mound behind the post office was

The sidewalk café was one of Santa Claus Land's dining options from the 1950s to 1970s. *Holiday World photo.*

promoted as the World's Largest Living Christmas Tree.

Until 1860, there were no cedar trees in the area, but some were brought to southern Indiana from the north. The Santa Claus Land tree was an offspring of one of the original cedars and was planted in 1890. While it was first decorated in 1946, it was not until the late 1950s when it emerged as its own attraction, decorated with one thousand plastic decorations and one thousand lights. The early October lighting was the official launch of the Christmas season. While the tree was a beloved landmark, disease prompted its removal in the 1970s.

As the fifties came to an end, Santa Claus Land started expanding its live entertainment offerings with Heinie's German Band performing in its own

gazebo in the park beginning in 1958. They were a Santa Claus Land staple for the next twenty years.

The next year, Willie Bartley's *Water Ski Thrill Show* debuted in Lake Rudolph where it operated for three seasons. A local resident, Willie Bartley, was inspired by the water ski shows in the Wisconsin Dells and recruited a group of local performers to put on their own performances. The group was best known for their "human kites."

In 1960, a "merger" took place that was critical to the future of Santa Claus Land when Bill Koch married Patricia Yellig, the daughter of Santa Claus (aka Jim Yellig). The couple waited until after Christmas, tying the knot on December 27, with the German Band providing the entertainment. Their first child, William Jr., was born the following year,

The Children's Roller Coaster was one of rides added in the 1960s as Pleasureland was expanded. *Holiday World photo.*

introducing a third generation to the park. Four siblings—Kristi, Dan, Philip, and Natalie—would follow.

Santa Claus Land continued to expand Pleasureland in the early 1960s with new rides including a children's roller coaster, kiddie Ferris wheel, the Duck and Goose ride, Jet Planes and a merry-go-round. Meanwhile, the Bavarian Glass Blowers, another longtime tradition, was added to the Main Lodge. Also, the park had switched to a pay-one-price admission, in which all attractions were free once the gate admission was paid. It is an industry standard today, but Santa Claus Land was one of the pioneers in offering it.

In 1965, several new features were added including the Seahorse kiddie ride, still a beloved attraction. A new transportation museum was opened in Lincoln Hall, a building that had served as a restaurant. The park had long had antique cars on display, and the new museum featured a variety of antique vehicles including a replica of a covered wagon, a surrey with the fringe on top, the stagecoach, which had been retired from its Pioneerland duty, and automobiles such as a 1916 Hudson, a 1926 Nash sports coupe, a 1926 model T, and a 1929 model A.

A new riverboat museum began a brief run, featuring a collection of twenty-four scale-models of riverboats that once plied the Ohio and Mississippi rivers and that were made by Colonel Geroge Borum of Centralia, Illinois. Throughout the park were arts and crafts demonstrations including the art of making candy and cookies, spinning yarn on a

A large merry-go-round joined the line up in Pleasureland during the 1960s. *Holiday World photo.*

Longtime employee Frieda Foertsch was involved with the Macaw Show, helped sew and repair Santa's suits, and eventually became known as the "flower lady" of the park. *Holiday World photo.*

spinning wheel, hand spinning of wool, and a display of handwoven textiles and rugs. By 1967, the park was promoting thirteen different exhibits including Pioneerland, Mother Goose Land, Toyland, House of Dolls, Circus, and the Nativity scene.

Live entertainment was taking on increased importance. Macaw shows became a staple, and for many years, "educated" animal shows were also a popular attraction. Provided by Animal Behavior Enterprises in Hot Springs, Arkansas, trained animals that performed tricks in exchange for a treat included a "kissing bunny," a "drumming duck," and a "baseball chicken." According to Will Koch, former president of Holiday World, the park had to have extra animals on hand because once an animal had eaten enough, they wouldn't perform.

As much as the park changed throughout the decade, the changes taking place surrounding Santa Claus Land were much more profound. In 1963, the park opened a campground to accommodate overnight visitors. Initially featuring eighty new campsites when it opened in June, it was expanded to two hundred sites by the end of the season, along with a full slate of modern amenities.

Bill Koch saw the success of Santa Claus Land as dependent on the success of the town of Santa Claus and knew it was critical for both to grow and succeed. In December 1965, he announced plans for a five-year, $3–$5 million expansion plan that would turn Santa Claus Land into the third-largest theme park in the United States, surpassed only by Disneyland and Six Flags Over Texas. But the largest component of this plan would not consist of attractions in the theme park; instead, it would be the development of a 1,500-acre residential development dubbed Christmas Lake Village, promoted as the place to build a second home

Christmas Lake Village was at the heart of Bill Koch's plans to grow not only Santa Claus Land but the entire community. *Holiday World photo.*

or retirement home. At the heart of the village was the 400-acre Christmas Lake, which would be created by constructing a 2,200-foot-long dam resulting in a lake 1.5 miles long with 10 miles of shoreline along which many of the homes would be located. The smaller Lakes Noel and Holly would be devoted to fishing and boating. Other recreational amenities would include a golf course, a swimming pool, bridle paths, and tennis courts.

But as the 1960s came to an end, Bill Koch was making plans for the future of Santa Claus Land. He envisioned new rides, displays, and gardens and foresaw the day where attendance would surpass one million. But to do that, Santa Claus Land had to change—change it did.

Growing Up—From Santa Claus Land to Holiday World

1970–1990

Jim Futrell

As the 1970s dawned, the United States was changing again. Baby boomers, the children of the World War II veterans who were so much a part of the founding of Santa Claus Land, were now starting families of their own. The nation's new interstate highway system allowed them to travel to more distant vacation destinations than their parents could, opening them up to whole new worlds of vacations.

The amusement park industry was changing too. The large urban traditional amusement parks that had dominated the industry when Santa Claus Land was founded had been fading away, falling victim to urban unrest, rising property values, aging facilities, and family succession challenges.

Around Santa Claus, Forest Park Highlands burned down in 1963, and Fontainne Ferry closed in 1969, never reopening following a riot in the park on opening day. Riverside Park followed in 1970, with Coney Island closing its cramped, flood-prone location in 1971. But that didn't mean that the amusement park industry was doomed—instead, it was evolving.

In the wake of Disneyland's success, entrepreneurs made several attempts to duplicate Walt Disney's vision. After several failed efforts, Six Flags Over Texas opened in 1961 between Dallas and Fort Worth.

With its suburban location right off the interstate highway, six themed lands, well-groomed spacious grounds, trained uniformed employees, family-oriented rides, and pay-one-price admission, Six Flags quickly became a favored destination, attracting 550,000 people in its first 45-day season.

The corporate-owned regional theme park was born. Throughout the 1960s and 1970s, a land rush ensued as developers sought to stake their claim in this exciting new industry, opening dozens of new attractions throughout the country on sites measuring hundreds of acres, located right off interstate highways in then-distant suburbs.

Following the success of their Texas park, Six Flags quickly followed suit with Six Flags Over Georgia in 1967 and, in 1971, Six Flags Over Mid-America outside St. Louis. In 1972, National Life Insurance and Accident Company, inspired by a 1969 visit by company executives to the year-old Astroworld theme park in Houston, developed a 120-acre parcel along the Cumberland River in Nashville into Opryland USA, the home of American music and the new location of the Grand Ole Opry. That same year, outside Cincinnati, Coney Island did not fade away like so many of its peers but moved many of its attractions to the massive new Kings Island,

Chronology

1975
Major expansion undertaken, adding the Reindeer Round Up Scrambler, Sunday Drivers bumper cars, Cloud Nine moonwalk, Spinning Drummer tubs, Snow Swirl kiddie whip, and Jonah's Whale

1976
Interstate Highway 64 is completed with an interchange just eight miles from Santa Claus. Santa Claus Land adds Wynken, Blynken, and Nod Tilt-A-Whirl and the Arctic Circle Round Up

1977
Theater and Flying Scooter added

1978
The Spider and Antique Cars make their debuts

1980
Thunder Bumpers bumper boats open

1981
Blitzen roller coaster installed

1983
In November, Santa Claus Land officially announces its transformation into Holiday World

1984
Holiday World opens. Many attractions are relocated and renamed, and the Frightful Falls log flume anchors the new Halloween section

1986
Banshee is added to Halloween

1988
26-year-old Will Koch, oldest child of Bill and Pat Koch, is named president of Holiday World

1990
Holiday World undertakes its largest project, Raging Rapids

Bill Koch (*third from right*) attending the bill signing officially moving Interstate 64 closer to Santa Claus.

Will Koch started working at Santa Claus Land in 1971 at 10 years of age. By 1974, he was hosting the Punch & Judy animal show. *Holiday World photo.*

developed by Taft Broadcasting. The opportunity presented by the regional theme park attracted a wide variety of companies. National Service Industries, a linen service company, purchased the shuttered Fontainne Ferry and reopened it in 1972 as Ghost Town on the River. But it was not a success and closed again in 1975.

Rather than view this new industry and its huge, new, well-funded competitors as a threat, Bill Koch embraced the opportunity to take Santa Claus Land to the next level and made plans for its future.

He knew that road access to the region was critical in enabling Santa Claus Land to fully reach its potential, and he was a big advocate for developing the area. He was a long-time proponent of a toll road that would travel from Owensboro, Kentucky, to Lafayette, Indiana. While it was never built, the completion of Interstate 64 through southern Indiana with an interchange just eight miles from

Santa Claus Land was his legacy. When the initial interstate highway map was released in 1956, it routed the Louisville to St. Louis segment of I-64 through Vincennes, Indiana, roughly forty miles to the north. Koch joined with other regional leaders to lobbying for a route closer to Santa Claus, eventually succeeding. In fact, Koch's role was considered so important that when it was completed in 1976, the dedication was held at the Santa Claus/Ferdinand exit.

While the 1970s began a little quieter for the park from an expansion perspective, the most critical development was the third generation of the Koch family starting to work at the park. A December 15, 1970, article in the Franklin *Daily Journal* mentioned that, "The Kochs, who have five children, also hope to interest them in the development of Santa Claus, just as Bill Koch was interested by his father, Louis J. Koch, of Evansville, now 89, to make the town a

The Children's Choir, seen here in 1970, was a longtime staple at Santa Claus Land. *Holiday World photo.*

Veteran circus performer Happy Kellems played the role of "official host" at Santa Claus Land in the 1970s, performing in shows and greeting guests. *Holiday World photo.*

lifetime career." Bill related in the article, "The oldest is only 9—William, Jr. But we can't keep them away from the place now. All five come here every day and the two oldest sing in the children's choir we have here every Sunday."

Will started working at the park the next year at ten years of age. His first job was to dress up in an elf costume. Then in 1974 he got promoted to overseeing the Punch and Judy show, a trained animal show featuring Miss Judy the chicken and Professor Punch the rabbit. He trained Punch to jump through a hoop and Judy to pull Punch out of a hat. By now, Santa Claus Land was promoting itself as the "Midwest's Largest Theme Park" with a season that had expanded from Easter to Christmas Eve.

In 1972, longtime entertainment anchors, the Santa Claus Children's Choir and the German Band, were joined by the Candy Cane Puppet Players and Happy Kellems, who played the role of Santa Claus

Land's official host for several years. A native of Evansville, Kellems career began as a performer in medicine shows in the early 1920s. Beginning with a Shrine Circus performance in Evansville in 1933, Happy developed his famous tramp character and toured with numerous circuses including Ringling Brothers and Barnum & Bailey Circus, Clyde Beatty Circus, Cole Brothers, and Sells-Floto. At Santa Claus Land, Kellems was joined by Gene Smith, a tap-dancing magician, at the Showboat Theater. Between shows he would wander around the park, greeting guests and doing what he loved the most—entertaining children.

Sixteen fantasy characters, seen here dancing in front of the bandstand, appeared at the park in 1974. *Holiday World photo.*

A Higher Profile

By now, construction of Interstate 64 was nearing completion, and Bill Koch was laying the groundwork to take advantage of the opportunity presented by the improved access. Summer had now emerged as the park's busiest season, and Koch saw their future as a bigger theme park. In an interview with the Owensboro, Kentucky, *Messenger*, he hinted at what was in store. "There are two schools of thought on the expansion. One is to do it all at once, the other is to spread it out over a period of time, so visitors will always come back to see what's new at Santa Claus Land."

"We're consulting architects and designers who drew up plans for some of the country's other theme parks. We've talked to some of the people that helped design Disneyland and the young man who did a lot of the work on Opryland."

Santa Claus Land emphasized its live entertainment offerings in 1974, promoting the new Punch and Judy trained animal show, sixteen strolling fantasy characters straight from Mother Goose, glass blowers, the Pied Piper marching band,

As Santa Claus Land started expanding in the 1970s, additional kiddie rides began to appear including Prancer's Merry-Go-Round. *Holiday World photo.*

The Reindeer Round Up Scrambler ride, seen in the background, was one of the first large rides to appear at Santa Claus Land. *Holiday World photo.*

and strolling musicians. Ads proclaimed, "The fun filled family park where the enchantment of Christmas reigns from Easter to Christmas Eve."

But while physical changes at the park were minimal, behind the scenes, big changes were afoot. After spending several years focusing on building up the surrounding town, Bill Koch knew the timing was right to really concentrate on expanding Santa Claus Land, and he kicked off a five-year expansion plan that would completely transform the park.

Knowing that his goal was to create an attraction that could compete with the large corporate theme parks springing up in the region around Santa Claus, Koch decided to bring in the best in the business to develop a master plan—Randall Duell.

A graduate of the University of Southern California School of Architecture, Duell started designing sets for Metro-Goldwyn-Mayer (MGM) in 1936 and ended up being an Academy Award–nominated set designer.

In 1959, he left MGM to join Marco Engineering, which was then designing Freedomland USA in the Bronx, one of the first and least successful attempts to copy the success of Disneyland.

Seeing the opportunity that existed in the emerging theme park industry, he established R. Duell and Associates in 1960. His training allowed him to combine traditional architecture with stagecraft to create elaborate themed lands. Starting with Six Flags Over Texas, Duell's firm went on to design most of the Six Flags parks, along with the Universal Studios Tour in California; Opryland; Hersheypark in Pennsylvania; and the Marriott Corporation's Great America theme parks in California and Illinois. By the time he went to work for Santa Claus Land, he was known as the world's leading theme park designer.

When guests arrived at Santa Claus Land in 1975, they were greeted by a number of new attractions. In

Above, As part of the 1975 expansion, the original Pioneerland train was retired and replaced with this new version. *Holiday World photo.*

Left, Santa Claus Land added a new front entrance as part of their 1976 expansion. *Holiday World photo.*

Pleasureland, the Reindeer Round Up, a Scrambler ride from the Eli Bridge Company of Jacksonville, Illinois, joined the kiddie rides. It was purchased from Mesker Park in Evansville, which was in the process of removing its amusement park rides. Next to the Hall of Famous Americans, a bumper car ride named Sunday Drivers debuted, and behind that was a new

kiddie area featuring four attractions—Cloud Nine, an inflatable moonwalk; Spinning Drummer, a Tubs of Fun ride; Snow Swirl, a kiddie whip; and Jonah's Whale, a rotating dipping whale ride better known as Bulgy. Rounding out the improvements were a new Pioneerland train manufactured by Chance Rides of Wichita, Kansas, and a new game room, located in the former toy warehouse.

By the next season, it was evident that a full-scale transformation from a kiddie-oriented park to a full-blown theme park was under way. Guests were greeted by a new front gate topped by a distinctive Christmas tree-shaped tower, eliminating the need to pay admission at the parking entrance. Next to

Sing Our Songs, America was the featured show in the park's new theater when it was built in 1977. Seen here is the 1990 edition. *Holiday World photo.*

Eagles Flight, a used Flying Scooter ride, was added in 1977. It remains a family favorite. *Holiday World photo.*

To make room for new attractions, Santa Claus Land retired the Deer Farm in 1976 and replaced it the next season with the Frontier Farm petting zoo. *National Amusement Park Historical Association archives—Tim O'Brien Collection.*

the new front entrance were two new rides. Wynken, Blynken, and Nod was a Tilt-A-Whirl also purchased from Mesker Park. Manufactured by Sellner Manufacturing of Faribault, Minnesota; the spinning, undulating ride is a staple in most amusement parks and carnivals. Next to that was Arctic Circle, a gravity-defying ride more popularly known as a Round Up. Santa Claus Land acquired it from Buckeye Lake Park in Ohio, another older amusement park that had closed.

Six shows were also added, including an equestrian act featuring a young Kristi Koch riding a horse through a flaming hoop, trained animals, a puppet show, a magician, and a clown show.

Finally, 950 new parking spaces were added that turned out to be needed. The two-year expansion program, coupled with the completion of Interstate 64, opened up Santa Claus Land to a whole new customer base, and attendance increased from 110,000 in 1975 to 165,000 in 1976.

Like its larger competitors, Santa Claus Land saw how important live entertainment was to attract the family market, and its major investment in 1977 was a $300,000 theater. Located next to the entrance, the 350-seat auditorium was outfitted with an elaborate multimedia system and recording equipment allowing a variety of entertainment to be presented.

The theater opened on June 25, presenting two daily performances of *Sing Our Songs, America.* The show was a forty-minute overview of American music touching on numerous genres including country-western, patriotic, rock, ragtime, and of course Christmas. The performers were 14 local college and high school students who went through a series of auditions the previous winter. They were directed and produced by David Girton, a former choral and drama director at South Spencer High School.

The ride lineup was expanded with the addition of a used Flying Scooter ride. Manufactured by Bisch Rocco, it gives riders the opportunity to control their own ride vehicle with the large wing mounted on the front of their car.

Rounding out the enhancements were five new carnival games, a large picnic area for the ever-growing group picnic business, and the Frontier Farm, a petting zoo featuring deer imported from Europe and trained by behavioral psychologists in Hot Springs, Arkansas, to respond to children.

Becoming Holiday World

Santa Claus Land, while transforming, was proving too limiting to hold all of Bill Koch's dreams. In a November 26, 1977, interview with *Amusement Business* magazine, Koch outlined his even grander plans for the park. "We're going professional. We're changing our image from basically a kiddie park to a major amusement park," admitting that the makeover had kicked off with the 1975 expansion, which helped to increase the average length of stay from just two hours in 1972 to five hours. He hinted that a ten-year growth plan would be launched in 1978.

At the time, the plan proposed that Santa Claus Land would remain the name of the park, because of the national publicity it generated. But hinting at what was to come, it was proposed that the park would become a "holiday land" with sections of the park themed to different holidays with possibilities including Halloween, Memorial Day, Independence Day, Saint Patrick's Day, and Lincoln's birthday. Attendance was projected to reach one million by 1988, more than four times their current visitation.

The ride line up continued to grow as the "Infamous" Spider and antique cars made their debuts for the 1978 season. Like most modern theme parks, rides and live entertainment began to define Santa Claus Land. Many of the static exhibits such as Pioneerland, the Transportation Museum, and the Miniature Circus that were so much a part of the park's early years were removed during this time.

The Antique Cars, now known as Lewis and Clark Trail, was built on the former location of the Deer Farm in 1978. *Holiday World photo.*

The Spider, installed in 1978, was renamed Paul Revere's Midnight Ride as part of Santa Claus Land's transformation. *Holiday World photo.*

When the Miniature Circus was retired around 1980, the building was converted into Skeeball Cottage. *National Amusement Park Historical Association archives—Tim O'Brien Collection.*

Thunder Bumpers provided a way to cool off before the bigger water attractions were added. *Holiday World photo.*

While Santa Claus Land's story continued to be one of constant growth, some traditions had ended. In 1977, for the first time since the park opened, the gates were locked in December. Winter business had been in decline for years, and the park cited increasing holiday promotions at malls as reducing people's desire to make the drive to Santa Claus. Also, since rides were a large part of park business, closing them down because of winter conditions made the park less appealing.

By 1979, more hints were being given about the future of Santa Claus Land. In a May 19, 1979, interview with the Jasper, Indiana, *Herald*, Bill Koch said, "The whole image of Santa Claus Land is going to be redone. We were the original theme park—with Santa Claus and Christmas. We've stayed with that, but we see we're too limited and we get too many misconceptions."

By 1988, Koch said, Santa Claus Land will become Holiday World, a community celebrating the major holidays of America. A first major step was completed in 1979 with the completion of Independence Plaza, an area devoted to the 4th of July and honoring Paul Revere's Midnight Ride, which became the new name of the Spider ride.

Even the park's news releases began stating "Santa Claus Land is more than a Christmas place. For more than three decades, it's been a holiday every day in a place called Santa Claus Land."

But not all of Koch's predictions proved to be accurate. At the time, he thought less and less emphasis would be placed on amusement rides. "We don't want to be in the battle of the biggest roller coaster. We're going to go for entertainment, beauty and I say educational—although I hesitate to call it that. We're going to use things a little bit historical, rides will be in the foreground, they won't be paramount."

The Thunder Bumpers bumper boat ride was the new attraction for the 1980 season, a water-based version of a bumper car ride in a 50-foot × 150-foot pond. But there were signs that something much bigger was on the horizon.

On December 21, 1980, an Indianapolis *Star* headline proclaimed, "Holiday World is the new

Blitzen was the park's first large roller coaster when it opened in 1981. *Holiday World photo.*

theme" in announcing the new direction of Santa Claus Land. "We're attempting to make Santa Claus Land into a major theme park in the Midwest," said Bill Koch. "We're the oldest theme park in the country, but we sat still in development while Disney and the others really moved. We're planning a major expansion during the next ten years in which we'll try to become as big as Kings Island or Six Flags at St. Louis are now. We have to do this on profits, cash flow and depreciation, so we might never be able to get as big as those parks, but at least we can close the gap." For the next few years, the Santa Claus Land name remained as the stage was set.

Since the Children's Roller Coaster was retired in the late 1960s, the park was lacking the most iconic of amusement park attractions—a roller coaster. That changed in 1981 when Blitzen opened. Purchased from Geauga Lake amusement park in

The ride was a family favorite during its seventeen seasons at the park. *Holiday World photo.*

Ohio and manufactured by Pinfari of Italy, the steel track ride stood 38 feet tall and featured 1,400 feet of track. Santa Claus Land decided to place it on one of the most high-profile locations on the property, a hill, surrounded by the train and at intersection of highways 162 and 245. It sent a powerful message that Santa Claus Land was changing. By early 1982, signs of a transformation were evident—rides were being moved and new food and games buildings erected.

Next came an upgrade to the old Pleasureland kiddie area in 1983, when the Thunder Bumpers Jr., a starter ride for the Thunder Bumpers would be added. It was the last ride that Santa Claus Land would add.

A Park Transformed

In November 1983, what had long been hinted at was now official—Santa Claus Land would be no more.

Aerial view or the transformed Holiday World in 1984. *Holiday World photo.*

The park was not closing but would be transformed through a multimillion dollar expansion program into Holiday World.

"We made the change for one particular reason—so many people looked upon it as Santa Claus Land. People who came to us under that name would continue, but the people who didn't come wouldn't. It's absolutely psychological. One lady told us that her husband would not come to the park as long as it was Santa Claus Land," Bill Koch told *Amusement Business* magazine in July 1984.

While Christmas would still be the park's heart and soul, it would now be joined by other themed areas celebrating other holidays.

When Holiday World opened in 1984, guests entered the park into the Christmas area where they were still greeted by the statue of Santa Claus. Nearby, Pleasureland was renamed Rudolph's

From Santa Claus Land to Holiday World

Transforming Santa Claus Land into Holiday World was a major multiyear undertaking that involved construction of new walkways, attractions, and buildings along with renaming and theming of existing features to fit in their new areas. Here is how the park changed from Santa Claus Land to Holiday World

Santa Claus Land, early 1980s	Holiday World, 1984
	Christmas theme area
Pleasureland kiddie area	Renamed Rudolph's Reindeer Ranch
Sky King	Renamed Blitzen's Airplanes
Neptune's Ponies	Renamed Dasher's Seahorses
All the King's Horses	Renamed Prancer's Merry-Go-Round
North Star	Renamed Comet's Rockets
Thunder Bumpers Jr.	Renamed Dancer
	New front entrance
	4th of July theme area—renovation of half of the original park plus newly built area
Arctic Circle	Relocated to 4th of July and renamed Roundhouse
Wynken, Blynken, and Nod	Relocated to 4th of July and renamed Virginia Reel
Mother Goose Land Train	Renamed Freedom Train
Spider	Renamed Paul Revere's Midnight Ride
Blitzen roller coaster	Renamed Firecracker
Antique Cars	Renamed Lewis and Clark Trail
Sunday Drivers bumper cars	Renamed Rough Riders
House of Dolls	Renamed Betsy Ross Doll House

Santa Claus Land, early 1980s	Holiday World, 1984
Stagecoach Theater	Renamed Stars and Stripes Theater
Magic Forest Theater	Renamed Town Crier Theater
Spinning Drummer	Renamed Pow Wow
Jonah's Whale ride	Renamed Salmon Run
Snow Swirl	Renamed Indian Dance

New Attractions

· Avenue of Flags
· Olympic Tryouts Games
· Funnel Cake and Ice Cream Factory
· Hoosier Hoedown Country Theater

Halloween theme area—newly constructed

Reindeer Round Up	Relocated to Halloween and renamed Scarecrow Scrambler

New Attractions

· Frightful Falls Flume
· The Spider's Web Games
· Merlin's Castle Arcade
· Pumpkin Plantation Restaurant

Above, The traditional heart of the park became the new Christmas-themed area. *Holiday World photo.*

Top right, 4th of July was the largest area and consisted of conversion of existing facilities and new construction. *National Amusement Park Historical Association archives— Tim O'Brien Collection.*

Right, The Roundhouse was originally added to the park as the Arctic Circle and moved to 4th of July as part of the transformation. *National Amusement Park Historical Association archives—Tim O'Brien Collection.*

Reindeer Ranch, with the five rides given seasonally appropriate names. The old Main Lodge was still home to a redecorated Christmas Dining Room and Toyland, while live entertainment was offered in the Holiday Theater. The Nativity scene was now the focus of a narrated musical presentation while the game room remained.

The remainder of the existing park was transformed into a new 4th of July area anchored by an Avenue of Flags displaying 20 variations of the American flag. The existing attractions remained although they were renamed to better reflect the spirit of the area.

But the original park only represented a portion of the new 4th of July area, which was the largest of the themed areas. A quarter-mile walkway loop was built through the woods, following the former Pioneerland train route that ran roughly from the antique auto ride, now called the Lewis and Clark Trail, to Rudolph's Ranch.

Along this route were the new home for the relocated Arctic Circle Round Up, now the Roundhouse, and the Wynken, Blynken, and Nod Tilt-A-Whirl, now called the Virginial Reel. Fourth of July was home to many of the park's live shows including a puppet show and macaw show, and next

Above, Live entertainment filled the transformed Holiday World including the *Macaw-lledge* bird show. *Holiday World photo.*

Top right, Halloween was a newly constructed themed area and home to the Holiday World's flagship ride. *National Amusement Park Historical Association archives—Tim O'Brien Collection.*

Right, Reindeer Round Up was relocated from the kiddie area to Halloween and renamed Scarecrow Scrambler. *National Amusement Park Historical Association archives—Tim O'Brien Collection.*

to Virginia Reel, the all-new Hoosier Hoedown Country Theater was constructed and featuring the *I Love Country Music* show.

Past the Hoosier Hoedown Theater, the new path extended to the newly constructed Halloween section which was located behind the Christmas section. The Reindeer Round Up was moved from the kiddieland

area and became the Scarecrow Scrambler. A new restaurant, Pumpkin Plantation, was added along with several games and an arcade.

These were only supporting players to the main attraction—the Frightful Falls log flume. Since the first version opened at Six Flags Over Texas in Arlington in 1963, the log flume had become one of

Left, Frightful Falls, an O. D. Hopkins log flume was the featured attraction at the newly transformed Holiday World. *National Amusement Park Historical Association archives—Tim O'Brien Collection.*

Below left, The ride culminated in a cooling 35-foot splashdown. *Holiday World photo.*

Below right, Banshee, a Chance Rides Falling Star, was the first ride added after the transformation to Holiday World. *Holiday World photo.*

High-dive shows became a popular attraction at Holiday World starting in 1986. *National Amusement Park Historical Association archives—Tim O'Brien Collection.*

the most popular rides at theme parks around the world, and Holiday World's decision to add one sent a powerful message about the future of the park.

Frightful Falls was built by O. D. Hopkins Associates of Contoocook, New Hampshire. The company was founded in 1962 as a manufacturer of ski lifts but later expanded into providing sky rides for amusement parks. Seeing that there was a market among smaller amusement parks for rides similar to the large spectacular attractions that characterized the big theme parks, Hopkins built its first log flume in 1980. Frightful Falls was Hopkins's tenth flume ride and featured a tunnel and a refreshing 35-foot drop along its 1,095-foot-long course. For people who didn't want to ride Frightful Falls, the Fright Chasm Overlook provided a view of the action.

"Holiday World, including the legendary Santa Claus Land" was promoted as "Bigger, brighter, more exciting than ever." Unfortunately, the start of season was hampered by poor weather and advertising challenges. Since the concept was so new, they had no images of the transformed park. But once they were able to start including footage of the flume, "It turned the tide literally," recalled Bill Koch. As a result, a 70 percent attendance drop in May was overcome, and by the time the park closed for the season, more than 250,000 people had come through the gates, more than 10 percent higher than in 1983.

Not only was the transformation to Holiday World in 1984 a milestone event, but also that year, the park and rest of the Santa Claus operations gained independence from George Koch Sons, the Evansville-based industrial company. This independence allowed Bill Koch to focus his full attention on the park and invest more heavily in expanding the operation.

Holidog Comes to Holiday World

From the park's earliest days as Santa Claus Land, people came to meet Santa Claus (as played by Pat Koch's father, Jim Yellig). Santa has remained a staple "character" to meet at the park ever since, but other characters have called Santa Claus Land their home over the years.

Bill Koch's sons had to play elves starting at about age ten. In one recollection, Will Koch remembered that the costumes were not very comfortable. Though growing up in a family-owned business and theme park such as Santa Claus Land could have many great perks, wearing a hot, itchy elf costume was not one of them! Still, the children that came to the park loved to meet with Santa and his elves, making for great family photo opportunities.

Over the years, other costumed characters made appearances at the park, including sixteen strolling fantasy characters straight from Mother Goose in the mid-1970s and the short-lived Merry Christmouse and Fun Deer.

But after Santa Claus Land transformed into Holiday World in 1984, the park added a new family-friendly show based on hit Broadway musicals called *On Broadway*. Lori Koch remembers the beginnings of what would become Holidog. "I think in 1985 or maybe '86. The original costume was used in our shows in 1984. It was supposed to be a generic knockoff of Snoopy. They went tan and brown instead of black and white. The show was *On Broadway*, and the

songs *Supper Time* and *Food, Glorious Food* were sung. *Supper Time* was from *You're A Good Man, Charlie Brown*, in which the dog character was used in that segment of the show."

Technically, this was not actually Holidog, at least not yet. However, the tan-and-brown dog with a baseball cap soon began to make public appearances in the park in 1985. Lori adds that at first, "There was never a mention of him being Holidog. I think Doug Weisheit may have come up with him? Really not sure. When I came back in 1987, he was here. I started the push for a better costume and design!" The name Holidog was first used to describe the character in 1985, and for 1988, Lori Koch had him totally redesigned by Scallon Productions into the lovable character that has become the official mascot of Holiday World ever since.

Since then, Holidog has been joined by other characters representing each of the different areas found in Holiday World. George the Eagle, an American bald eagle caricature wearing patriotic attire represents 4th of July; Kitty Klaws, a tutu-wearing black cat with masquerade mask can be found greeting children in Halloween; and Safari Sam is a friendly crocodile wearing an Australian-style explorer hat and beach gear while hanging out in the Splashin' Safari water park. All of these characters, along with Santa Claus himself, help to bring smiles to children of all ages and make for some unforgettable memories and photo opportunities.

Right, Holidog began performing in stage shows starting in 1985 before transforming into the beloved mascot he is today. *Holiday World photo.*

Below, Holidog, seen here with the short-lived mascot Fun Deer, has evolved since his debut. *Holiday World photo.*

Halloween saw another new attraction in 1986 when Banshee opened. Generically known as a Falling Star, Banshee was manufactured by Chance Rides of Wichita, Kansas, one of the country's largest ride manufacturers. The 66-foot-tall ride was the first one in the region and quickly became a guest favorite with its "over-the-top" sensation resulting in falling at a rate of 32 feet per second, exerting 2.5 g's of force in the process. The ride was named for a legendary ethereal spirit that wails and screams uncontrollably at the prospect of one's immediate gruesome fate. The screams that Banshee generated from riders made it fit the atmosphere of Halloween perfectly.

Next to Frightful Falls, the Great American High Diving show made its debut. The action-packed shows featured stunts such as a 45-foot-high dive and a human torch and became a longtime favorite at the park. It also signaled more elaborate entertainment productions coming to the growing park. The following season, Holidog made his official debut as the park mascot after appearing in stage shows since 1985.

In 1988, the *Chinese National Acrobats of Taipei*, including acrobats, jugglers, contortionists, and magicians debuted. To accommodate the acrobats, the 1,400-square-foot stage in the Holiday Theater had to be lowered by three and a half feet at a cost of $50,000, but due to the language barrier, they had a communication issue and ended up having to raise 225 square feet back to the original level. By now the park had six theaters, presenting nine different shows. The show production budget for the year totaled $200,000.

SantaFest offered visitors horse and carriage rides through the grounds. *Holiday World photo.*

Christmas Carolers added to the festive mood at SantaFest. *Holiday World photo.*

Passing the Torch

As the 1988 season wound down, Bill and Pat Koch's oldest son Will Koch was named president of Holiday World at twenty-six years old, signaling the beginning of a transition to the third generation of the family. But the couple remained very much a part of the operation, with Bill continuing to serve in a consulting capacity.

Anyone who has visited Holiday World in July or August knows, it can be a very hot place. To combat that, the park added "outdoor air conditioning" in 1989 in hopes of increasing stays in hot weather. Installed in the Halloween section of the park, the MEE II Cloud Make System was capable of lowering the temperature in an open outdoor area by up to thirty degrees by generating a cloud of microscopic water droplets that evaporate when released in the air. As an added benefit, the fog fit into the theme of the Halloween section.

At the end of 1988, Holiday World opened its Christmas section for one weekend in December to see how the public would respond to a new holiday

season. The popularity of that weekend resulted in the launching SantaFest.

Starting the first three days after Thanksgiving, and running the first three weekends of December, only the Christmas section of the park was open. Highlights included a living nativity, Old English Carolers strolling through the park, Santa Claus, thirty-four arts and crafts exhibits from craftsmen throughout Indiana and Illinois, carriage rides, kiddie rides in Rudolph's Reindeer Ranch, the bumper cars, Freedom Train, and *A Christmas to Remember*.

This was a musical show centered around a grandfather who gives each child a personal treasure from the past, sharing memories of that item. In retrospect, SantaFest was a bit ahead of its time. While more and more theme parks throughout the country are now open over the holiday season, it proved difficult for Holiday World to attract enough people to Santa Claus in the winter, and it was discontinued after 1991.

As Holiday World entered the 1990s, it was truly a transformed park. In a little over a decade, the park had grown from a roadside kiddie attraction

Will Koch's wife Lori performed in the feature show at SantaFest—*A Christmas to Remember*. *Holiday World photo.*

In 1989, Santa joined Will and Bill Koch to break ground on Raging Rapids. *Holiday World photo.*

to a growing regional theme park. Increasing crowds meant the need to add bigger rides, and the 1990 season was highlighted by the park's largest investment to date—Raging Rapids—Will Koch's first big project.

Raging Rapids was a river rapids ride that simulated the adventure of whitewater rafting. The concept was developed in the late 1970s by Bill Crandall, general manager of Six Flags Astroworld in Houston, who was inspired by Olympic kayaking races. He worked with Swiss manufacturer Intamin to develop the concept and the first ride opened at Astroworld in 1980. The sensation of floating down river rapids not quite knowing who on the boat would get soaked was an immediate sensation and theme parks throughout the world started adding them.

Holiday World returned to Hopkins, which started manufacturing river rapids in 1988, for their version.

The three-minute ride was 1,182 feet long and featured a 9.5-foot elevation change and a speed of 11 feet per second. The ride begins with a 200-foot-long tunnel into a small lake lined with eight geysers shooting water 20 feet in the air. While six were automatically activated, two geysers are coin operated by park visitors from an observation platform. The ride then travels through twisting paths of boulders and trees.

The grand finale is a ride through the abandoned town of Boulder Canyon, which according to legend,

Raging Rapids recreated an outdoor rafting adventure in a previously undeveloped area of the park. *Holiday World photo.*

was destroyed by an earthquake and flood in the 1880s. Boats float down the flooded main street and into the Saloon where cowboy hats bob in the water and a player piano still plays.

But even after completing as big a project as Raging Rapids, Holiday World made numerous other improvements. For smaller children, Indian River (now Tippecanoes), a kiddie canoe ride, replaced the Pow Wow spinning tubs ride. Meanwhile, a new show lineup debuted throughout the park. In addition, the Frontier Farm was redesigned as a stroll through habitat with kiosks for petting and feeding animals. With crowds growing, Holiday World began staying open until 10 p.m. for the first time in its history, which turned out to be needed as attendance grew by more than 12 percent to 314,000.

The addition of Raging Rapids truly represented a "watershed" for Holiday World. It demonstrated once and for all that it was no longer the small roadside kiddie park that so many remembered but had grown into a true regional theme park. It was now adding large amusement rides and making a major commitment to add water-based attractions. This portended the true emergence of the Holiday World known around the world today.

Still ranked among the most popular rides at Holiday World, Raging Rapids set a new standard for future Holiday World attractions. *Jim Futrell photo*.

Recollections

Special Moments at and about Holiday World & Splashin' Safari

Compiled by Ron Gustafson

John Wood, chairman and CEO, Sally Dark Rides/ Sally Corporation, Jacksonville, Florida

"We had been friends with the Kochs for a long time, and they had an open desire to have a dark ride. As it turned out, the Thanksgiving area (in Holiday World) was the place, but we could not shoot the turkeys. Our creative designer at the time, Drew Hunter (Drew is now vice president of creative design at Sally) started working on a concept in which the turkeys escaped and all of the town's people got together and used turkey callers to round them up."

That was the beginning of Gobbler Getaway, a family-friendly themed interactive dark ride that opened in 2006. It is in a blacklight setting, and guests use the electronic turkey callers to round up the missing flock while scooting along in four-passenger cars.

"There's a granny in the queue line (Abigail) who tells the story about the event 100 years ago."

John Wood also sat on the attractions and amusement industry's Applause Award Board of Governors when he was approached by the late Will Koch regarding the esteemed honor, which is given to one park in the world every two years.

"Will, in particular, said we (board) should take a hard look at a small park with the right personality, cleanliness, and quality service to compete against the large parks that had always won," Wood noted. "At that time, Holiday World was a jewel as polished as it could be."

Holiday World won the award for 2004–2005.

Lori Gogel, director of revenue administration, Holiday World & Splashin' Safari

"I first visited the park in 1993 and the following year decided I wanted to work there. I started in the water park as a lifeguard and went full time in 1997, when I was promoted to director (1997–2014). Wildebeest is still my favorite (water park ride), and I worked extensively with Will and ProSlide in building it. I sat in on the meetings and pointed out things we wanted. I remember the day Will passed—he spent a lot of time watching it that day. He had the biggest grin—he was so excited, and he said to me 'What's next?'"

"We've always had a vision of looking at 'families first.' An example was in 2011 we put in Safari Sam's Splashland. I had more people that year stop me and thank me for putting in a kiddie pool. I was just overwhelmed by how many folks came up to me."

Rick Emmons, graphic artist, Holiday World & Splashin' Safari

"I've been at the park 45 years, going on 46. I started out in high school in grounds mowing and that kind of stuff—did a little bit of everything. I did some art school training and came back and started painting statues for the summer at the park. To stay on here I painted rides, buildings—everything that needed it—and ended up being the paint shop manager. I still do some graphics. I'm a chief cook and bottle-washer of sorts."

"In the late '80s when Will took over, I got so busy that I asked if I could do graphics full time. They did a series of Christmas murals, seven or eight of them, and that's when I requested I go into graphics, and I've stayed on it from that point. There are thousands of signs in the park today, some creative and elaborate. Thunderbird (roller coaster) was a big job, and Cheetah Chase—last year—was really nice. Pretty much today the signs are a combination of hand-cut vinyl and paint. We're also halfway through painting the carousel menagerie animals—a zebra, dragon and horses. It's a massive project with inlaid jewels. Trying to get the right jewel replacements for those is hard as they are oddball sizes. Kind of fun, but a challenge. And we're doing everything else at the same time, trying to fit that in. That's [carousel animals] all airbrush and brush work."

"I think back at the days when Will was here. He was always out (in the park) and also very complimentary of my work. It's a great place to work and the Koch family—having a direct connection with the owners no matter what you did. No job to them was too small."

"Joe Hevron worked here for fifty years. He passed away but worked here until he was probably 80, collecting the cash and he took it to the bank every day. A gift shop near the Thunderbird has his name: Hevron's Mercantile. I have no plans of retiring and I'm 65."

Ed Janulionis, sales manager, Allan Herschell Company, North Tonawanda, New York

"Those rides from the 1940s, '50s and '60s were indestructible. Thank God—if it wasn't for that I wouldn't be in business."

"Those kiddie rides built by Herschell were representative of what was going on in the world at the time. The jeep and tank rides came out during the Korean War. The helicopter ride closely mimicked Bell Aerospace's helicopter. Bell was located in nearby Niagara Falls at the time. Herschell was very clever in that respect as these kiddie rides were interactive with bells, buzzers and steering wheels. I service 15 different rides from that era."

The Allan Herschell Company was once the largest manufacturer of amusement rides in the nation, and Holiday World operates a kiddie ride it calls the Comet's Rockets, which is a 1950 Herschell Sky Fighter. Holiday World acquired the ride—likely from another operator—in the 1970s, according to the park's timeline. Holiday World, operating as Santa Claus Land during its early years, was also home to a Herschell Little Dipper roller coaster, Blue Goose ride, merry-go-round, and kiddie boat ride. Comet's Rockets is likely the oldest operating ride in the park.

Tim O'Brien, amusement industry journalist

"I had been to Holiday World on several occasions, covering events and new attractions, and got to know Will Koch and his family. Will called me out of the blue one day when I was still working at *Amusement Business* (trade publication) and said they were thinking about building a big woodie (roller coaster) and wondered if I would come up to the park."

"We took a golf cart out and started walking through the woods. Will would point out a feature on the coaster—all of this in his head—and the way he talked it would be a wild coaster in the Halloween section of the park. And Will said, 'What do you think?' I said I can just see people getting off the coaster yelling 'Never more, never more' from Edgar Allan Poe's poem "The Raven." And by golly, first thing I know I get a note from the park saying 'Thanks, we're going to call it The Raven.'"

A plaque on the The Raven acknowledges Tim O'Brien as suggesting the name of the iconic ride.

"On another occasion, we were with an association group visiting the Netherlands in the '90s and doing some walking to see the countryside. As I took a shortcut across a lawn, Will saw me and yelled 'Duck, Tim, duck!' as a windmill blade missed me by inches. The only thing I got out of it was two grass-stained knees."

Interesting note about The Raven from the park's website: the name "The Raven" was chosen for our first wooden coaster exactly 145 years to the day following the death of Edgar Allan Poe. The poem "The Raven" was first published in 1845; our coaster by the same name premiered 150 years later, in 1995. Ravens used to thrive in Indiana. The last sighting of ravens nesting in southern Indiana was in 1894. This was exactly 100 years before construction of The Raven roller coaster began in the town of Santa Claus, Indiana

Leah Koch, director of communications and fourth-generation owner, Holiday World & Splashin' Safari

"The Raven opened in 1995 and I was 4 going on 5 at the time and an abnormally tall child, so I fit the height requirement to ride. But I was afraid to go on a roller coaster. The Raven had a single lap bar for both people, and I went on with Dad. He told Paula (public relations director at the time) that I shrank down in the seat, and he held on to me, though I don't recall that. I did ride and hated it—did not like it at all."

"In early 2000 we built The Legend [coaster], and Dad took us straight over to the park after karate lessons to ride it before anyone else did. By that time, I was getting more confident of it (riding). Actually, I was a Skeeball queen."

"When I was young, we had a birthday party and our parents allowed us to walk on the Skeeball lanes, which was a huge no-no, so we could drop the balls into the holes."

"Spring was always fun when we had a new ride because we would think, hey, we're going to fire this thing up. And if Dad showed up at school, we knew we were going to ride something new."

"When The Voyage (roller coaster) started running, I didn't get pulled out of school but let other people ride first because I had to study for math."

Eric Snow, vice president and chief marketing officer, Holiday World & Splashin' Safari

"I started seasonally in 1998 as a ride operator and did that for three years and was also a marketing intern under John Chidester. A few years after college, I worked at the Indianapolis Zoo but have been full time at the park since 2007. I was director of admissions after coming back, then worked on special events and projects for the shoulder season before being promoted to my current role."

"Everything that happens at Holiday World comes out of our little office. We've put a lot of value in our tickets with free soda and sunscreen and our guests spread the word to others. We're very innovative and not afraid to try new things and our focus is on the long term—taking care of our guests and making sure the experience we are delivering is long-term. That is our culture. The bulk of people visiting the park drive from three hours away."

Right, Holiday World founder Louis J. Koch and Santa hosted future President Ronald Reagan in 1955.

Below right, Will Koch visiting with Santa (aka his grandfather Jim Yellig). *Holiday World photo*.

Above, Koch family Christmas card in 1969 with (*from left*) Will, Dan, Philip, Kristi, and Natalie.

Left, Pat Koch poses with her four oldest children and her father Santa Jim. *Clockwise from top*: Will, Dan, Philip, and Kristi. *Holiday World photos*.

Clockwise from top left, Growing up, Will Koch could count on the advice of Santa (aka his grandfather Jim Yellig). *Holiday World photo*; Will and Bill Koch with Santa in 1987. *National Amusement Park Historical Association Archives—Tim O'Brien Collection*; Will Koch and Holidog at work. *Holiday World photo*; Lori and Lauren Koch in the Frontier Farm. *Holiday World photo*.

Clockwise from top left, Lauren, William, and Leah Koch with Holidog; Will and Lauren Koch try out Congo River ; Pat and Will Koch in Splashin' Safari; Lauren Koch poses in front of the plaque commemorating Holiday World's 45th Anniversary. *Holiday World photos.*

Clockwise from top left, Lauren Koch with her grandfather Bill; Bill and Pat Koch trying out the new Legend train at the 1999 IAAPA trade show; William Koch in front of the new Holiday World water tower. *Holiday World photo.*

"The greatest thing about Holiday World for me is that all of our employees are young and learn work ethic here—how to work with people, manage people, and work with money. It's amazing to see how many have worked here and move on to better jobs. I fell in love with this place and the industry and found it hard to leave."

Don Baggett, magician, Holiday World & Splashin' Safari

"My first vacation as a ten-year-old kid was to Santa Claus Land (Holiday World)—thirty minutes from my house. I sat there all day and watched the magic show, and I remember telling my mom I wanted to some day be the magician at Santa Claus Land. She got me a magic show for Christmas that year."

Don started his eighth season as the park's magician in 2021.

"Decades later, here I am where it all started. I'm so blessed to be able to do this! The relationships you make with the people you work with, the park owners, and the guests after the shows—that's the best thing about working in this industry. For me, taking that final bow on the stage and you know you have touched them (audience) and there is no substance that can create that for me."

"I was wearing white sleeves one day and the rabbit I was using in the show scratched me—at least I thought so. I continued on with the show and then I noticed kids started gawking at me. Then I noticed crimson (blood) coming through the sleeve. Thank goodness it was Halloween season and I told them it was all part of the show."

"There was a little boy that would come to every show. He was autistic. In 2017 he was there before we closed for the final show. I walked out and brought him up on stage and he did everything perfectly! He's still my friend and that is a memory I will always cherish."

Matt Blumhardt, vice president and chief operating officer, Holiday World & Splashin' Safari

"I started working at Cedar Point (theme park in Sandusky, Ohio) when I was seventeen, which was understandable as I was always obsessed with amusement parks. I never heard of Holiday World but in 2009 came here with a friend. Little did I know that nine years later I would see a position posted at Holiday World for vice president of revenue. I was at Worlds of Fun in Kansas City at that time. I knew Holiday World was highly regarded in the industry, family owned and a smaller park. Had I not made that trip with my friend, I would never have looked at this job—that trip was pivotal."

"I started working with Leah Koch in revamping the food and beverage pricing and that's how we got to know each other. We both have a passion for the business and see eye-to-eye on a lot of things. She has a passion that her dad had. I'm a revenue guy, but Holiday World showed me that you can make really good money without nickel and diming people. We give them free parking, free soda, free sunscreen—those things come from what Leah's dad put into place. Once you are in the gate here it is carefree."

COVID-19 and the ensuing pandemic impacted business worldwide, but—perhaps—no industry was hurt as much as the theme park business by the health crisis.

"We were geared up for what would have likely been a record season in 2020. We were poised, had the momentum and then COVID happened. Our team did such a great job maneuvering through it. I think it was our finest moment. To stand at the front gate and watch those first guests come in was a special moment."

"Sometimes you feel that you are meant for something, and this is it. I love this job."

Matt Eckert, president and chief executive officer, Holiday World & Splashin' Safari

"I worked in public accounting right out of college. I had a friend in college who worked here, and he called me and said Holiday World was looking for a controller. I met with Will Koch and within the first five minutes we clicked and I was sold. He called me the next day and offered me the job and I took it. I've been here twenty-one years."

Matt also served as one of the park's two general managers from 2007 to 2012. In 2013, the park's board of directors named him as president and CEO.

"Will was one of my best friends and he still lives with us. He truly was a pioneer in the industry, and he did so much for me personally. I remember when he brought up the idea of free soft drinks. I thought he was crazy, but it worked. Will was a good crazy."

"We make laughter and that's so important, especially now when people need to find joy in their lives. And that's what we do. At the end of the day when you see those kids and families leaving with smiles on their faces, ice cream on their lips, that's one of the best things about our business."

"We don't know the story of everyone coming through the gate, but I remember we got a photo of a family emailed to us and a note that the father had cancer and wanted to come to Holiday World. They came and he passed away a week later. They (family) cherished that time together—it was a heartwarming moment. It brings you joy knowing you were able to do that for them."

"If you asked me twenty-five years ago what I would be doing and you told me I would be president of a theme park, I would have told you you were crazy. Now I can't imagine doing anything else."

Korey Kiepert, member/manager, The Gravity Group, Cincinnati, Ohio

"When I was in college, I was part of ACE (American Coaster Enthusiasts) and I remember reading *Roller Coaster* magazine when it compared The Raven (Holiday World) to The Beast (Kings Island, Cincinnati) and saying it was a must-ride roller coaster. We went to one of the first *Stark Raven Mad* events and I remember driving into the parking lot and thinking, 'Wow, I drove all night for this?' It wasn't very impressive to look at, but I rode it and was blown away. There was a walkback tour that day and I talked to Mrs. Koch and told her I wanted to design coasters some day."

Korey joined Custom Coasters International after the firm built Holiday World's coaster The Legend, which opened in May of 2000. In 2002, The Gravity Group was formed by the engineering team that worked at Custom Coasters, which went out of business. In 2006, the park introduced *The Voyage*, a massive coaster designed by The Gravity Group.

"Though I wasn't involved in the design of The Legend, Michael Graham and I had the pleasure of going out shortly after it opened. I remember being selected because we were the newest, youngest people at Custom Coasters. Will (Koch) wanted to speed up the train on that ride as he was adamant about it making a good first impression. You know, amusement parks can be a little creepy at night, and The Legend had a sensor on the lift hill which prompted a message: 'Don't Look Back!' That would come on in the middle of the night, but it added to the fun of working there. We got the job done in a couple of nights. Both of us came out covered with grease."

"One of our first jobs at The Gravity Group was to work with Holiday World. They wanted to make The Raven into the two-train operation it is today. We did the engineering, and the park did the rest."

"Will wanted to be involved in the design of The Voyage, and Will is listed as such. The return run on The Voyage zigzags around—dodging in and out of the structure. We always felt that Holiday World was very supportive of our company."

DeeAnn Woolems, accounting manager, Holiday World & Splashin' Safari

"I started as group sales coordinator in 1993, left for a year and a half, and came back to group sales. We didn't have a call center at that time and worked out of a double-wide trailer we called the 'spacious double-wide.' In essence it was our marketing office at the time. We held marketing meetings at the kitchen table. I remember filling out handwritten season passes at the time—even on my kitchen table at home. We had documents stored in the bathtub in that office, and one day we had a newscaster in there trying to simulate our high-diving team. He put a coffee cup filled with water on the floor and stood on the kitchen counter to give the perspective of what high divers see looking down from the platform."

"I went to Will (Koch) and asked if he could find something else for me and he found a purchasing position that transitioned into accounting, and I have been doing this (finance) since 2008. Will and I were classmates in high school and that sort of helped."

"Will would just pop by my office and say, 'Happy Tuesday.' He would look out his door and see the traffic coming into town and gauge what attendance would be for that day. Though I didn't work here, like a lot of high school students, I worked at a grocery store in town. I grew up here and was part of the Santa Claus Land children's choir."

Rick Hunter, chairman and chief executive officer, ProSlide Technology, Ottawa, Ontario, Canada

"Number one is family. It's all about family at Holiday World—the way they treat their guests and welcoming them back. And the Koch family; they are absolutely team members, and they took that thinking into their supply chain."

ProSlide Technology has been involved with all of the major water slide projects at Holiday World & Splashin' Safari for 20 years. The ProSlide installments at the park have won numerous industry honors over the years.

"My background is ski racing and mountains and before I started ProSlide, I worked on Alpine slides—you know the ones where you ride on a cart down the mountainside in the summer. I remember when Will Koch and I were looking around the park for a place for what would be Watubee (opened in 1996). I said we can custom design one to fit underneath one of these wooden roller coasters. It turned out to be amazing and created interaction between the water park and the ride park."

"I would go out every time Will would phone, and in 2002, we opened ZOOMbabwe. It's the highest enclosed dark water slide—an amazing ride. Will and I were there together when we opened Wildebeest (2010). Everybody couldn't believe it. Even the roller coaster guys were impressed by this."

Wildebeest was the world's longest water coaster when it opened and utilized linear induction motor technology to propel four-person boats up hills and through tunnels.

"Every time I would visit, someone would say 'There goes Rick and Will into the woods again.' (scouting for new water slide locations). We all miss Will and talk about a love for that park. We're (ProSlide) entrepreneurs like the Kochs. We were a match made in heaven."

Michael Crosby, director of games operations, Holiday World & Splashin' Safari

"It was a life-altering experience my first year at the park in 2010. I was new to the theme park business and my wife's dad (late Will Koch) opened his heart and home to me. He changed my whole perspective in terms of working to serve others—he redirected my life."

"One guy comes to the park every year to play our three-point (basketball) game. He travels to all of the parks to play, and he plays and wins. Maybe he has a love for the game, maybe it's an addiction. Some years he spends more on the game than he wins. We have some nice prizes including TVs and home video games."

"The most fulfilling part of my job is seeing kids win at our games. They're so happy, and it's really rewarding to see that. We're not selling games, we're selling memories—that is our job to make someone's day brighter."

Lauren Crosby, director of entertainment and events and fourth-generation owner, Holiday World & Splashin' Safari

"I can literally take a step out of my office and hear people laughing and screaming—making incredible memories. We help make that for them."

"My sister, Leah, and I both performed in the park's shows during our school years. I was backstage during one show when a zipper on my costume broke. Leah stayed onstage and finished the show without me."

"In May of 2019 we were about to open for our season pass preview night. A girl comes across the midway with a giant tub of funnel cake batter, and she dumped it. It couldn't be cleaned up quick enough, so we had to stop there and block it while waving and saying 'Hi' to everyone as they came in."

"I was in high school the week my dad was testing The Voyage. Every morning I would wonder: is today the day? We knew the day was coming when Dad would come to school and pull us out so we could ride it. We checked our class schedules to see what was a good time and day to skip out of school to go ride the new roller coaster. Who else gets to sit at the breakfast table and ask your dad when do you get to ride the new roller coaster?"

William Koch III, director of technical production and fourth-generation owner, Holiday World & Splashin' Safari

"I worked with my dad when I was young, and he helped me find things to do around the park and learn different aspects of the business. I wanted to learn as much as I could. When I was 14, I went into cash control and entertainment as a sound technician. That's (sound) what I do now and definitely enjoy it."

"Mom took me on The Raven (roller coaster) when I was young, and I actually remember crying about getting on it. When I got off, I said, 'Let's do it again!'"

On another occasion, "We were staging photos on the brake run of the roller coaster and the photographer was having a hard time getting the shot. I was terrified and sitting there crying. They got me to stop crying long enough to get a photo."

"What I enjoy the most about the industry is the people—those I work with, friends in the industry we see at trade shows and meeting new ones during networking."

Nevermore and Forever— Holiday World Reaches New Heights

1990–2010

Dave Hahner

Although the park dates back to 1946, few people outside of southern Indiana and northern Kentucky were familiar with the park whether as Santa Claus Land or even Holiday World in the early 1990s. It was still very much a small regional theme park that was extremely popular to its local fan base. But Bill and Pat Koch and their children had other ideas. The park was ready for a change, a very BIG change during this formative decade that would put Holiday World on the map forever. Amusement park and roller coaster enthusiasts from around the world would soon travel to the sleepy little town known as Santa Claus, Indiana. Two major factors would play a part in this. The first dealt with water, lots of water with the addition of the Splashin' Safari water park. The other would deal with wood, lots and lots of wood as a manmade "forest" of wood and steel would soon permeate the skyline of the park, changing the course of Holiday World forever.

After the very successful addition of Raging Rapids in Boulder Canyon, the focus would primarily be centered on the addition of the new for 1993 water park, which became known as Splashin' Safari. The rest of the park was given overall aesthetic improvements to handle the expected larger crowds during this period, including the all-new Kringle's Kafé in 1991. As the park's largest eating facility, located in the Christmas section, the huge new cafeteria-style restaurant, which specialized in pizza and sandwiches, cost well over $1 million to construct. A new ride addition to the park the following year was an upcharge attraction known as Stormin' Norman's Tank Tag which was added to the 4th of July section. The attraction was named after General "Stormin'" Norman Schwarzkopf, leader of the American and Allied forces during the 1991 Operation Desert Shield, later to become the Operation Desert Storm offensive to help liberate Kuwait after the invasion by Iraq. Riders would sit in a small-scale replica of an army tank where they could shoot tennis balls with air guns at each other. If the target on the side of the tank was hit, it would

Chronology of Holiday World 1991–2009

1991
Kringle's Kafé added to Christmas

1992
Kid's Castle and Deer Playground added to Rudolph's Reindeer Ranch in Christmas, Stormin' Norman's Tank Tag added to 4th of July

1995
The Raven wooden coaster added to Halloween, first *Stark Raven Mad* event held for roller coaster enthusiasts

1997
Firecracker steel roller coaster removed

1999
Holidog's Funtown area was added within the loop of Freedom Train/Mother Goose Land, including Howler family coaster and Doggone Trail jeep ride

2000
The Legend wooden roller coaster added to Halloween, Free Unlimited Soft Drinks begins, first Pepsi Oasis to offer free drinks was built in Halloween

2001
Bill Koch passes away at age 86

2002
Banshee (Chance Falling Star ride) is retired

2003
HallowSwings (Halloween-themed Zamperla Flying Trapeze) added to Halloween, replacing Banshee, Liberty Launch (Double Shot tower from S & S Worldwide) added to 4th of July, replacing Hall of Famous Americans

2004
Holiday World & Splashin' Safari wins the prestigious Applause Award

2005
Revolution (Hrubitz Round Up ride) replaced the park's original Roundhouse Round Up ride, Virginia Reel (original Sellner Tilt-A-Whirl) was retired

2006
New Thanksgiving section added to Holiday World includes The Voyage wooden roller coaster designed by The Gravity Group and Gobbler Getaway, Sally Corporation, interactive dark ride

2007
Plymouth Rock Café featuring full-course Thanksgiving style turkey dinners and Turkey Whirl (new turkey-themed Sellner Tilt-A-Whirl) also added to Thanksgiving

2008
Star Spangled Carousel (Chance carousel) added to 4th of July, replacing Thunder Bumper bumper boat attraction

2009
Pilgrim's Plunge, world's tallest flume ride, from Intamin of Switzerland, was added to Thanksgiving (renamed Giraffica in 2013)

immobilize the tank temporarily while the opponent could continue to attack. Coin-operated guns on the sides of the arena allowed guests to also participate and try to shoot the tanks. The interactive attraction only lasted through the end of the 1996 season.

The Raven Takes Flight

At this point, the Splashin' Safari water park received the most investment, and for good reason as park attendance began to steadily increase since its opening in 1993. But Bill and Will Koch's ambitions were for something large for Holiday World too. Will Koch was determined to put a major roller coaster into Holiday World for the park's fiftieth season in 1995. He was a huge fan of The Beast wooden roller coaster at Kings Island theme park in Mason, Ohio, near Cincinnati. That ride, the world's longest wooden roller coaster, fascinated Will. He loved the wooded setting and the coaster's numerous signature elements, especially the massive tunneled double helix finale. Will wanted a somewhat similar, yet unique, world-class wooden roller coaster for Holiday World, and he wanted it by 1995 to help celebrate the park's fiftieth season of operation.

Will met up with Denise Dinn Larrick, president and owner of Custom Coasters International (CCI) of West Chester, Ohio, in summer 1993. CCI was the premier wooden roller coaster design company during this time, known for some great medium-sized wooden coasters such as Outlaw at Adventureland in Altoona, Iowa, and Hoosier Hurricane at Indiana Beach, Monticello, Indiana. Denise was the daughter of Charles Dinn, the man who helped to build and design the monstrously famous and popular The Beast for Kings Island. After seeing what CCI was capable of doing, they sent a survey team of engineers to the park to determine what site to build the coaster on. Will wanted something that would be built in

the woods utilizing as much of the park's natural terrain as possible, very similar to how The Beast was designed. He also knew where he wanted the coaster to be built—near the front gate so arriving guests could marvel at the new coaster. It was also decided that a spectacular turnaround would be built over a section of the park's largest body of water, Lake Rudolph.

CCI engineers Larry Bill and Dennis McNulty were assigned with the not-so-simple task of creating this new wooden coaster that would actually be a part of the Halloween section of the park. Not to mention the added pressure that Will Koch wanted the coaster to be one of the best in the world! McNulty recalls crawling through the heavily wooded terrain getting covered in ticks as they scoped out the topography of the area. Several design concepts were created by Bill and McNulty. Will Koch liked one design utilizing the natural slopes of the area and the high-speed diving turn toward Lake Rudolph. However, one of the earlier designs had the coaster simply just return to the brake run with a series of high-speed "bunny hops" back to the station. Will Koch had other plans. Not only did he want a more intense and fun experience, but he also wanted to save as many large trees as possible along the coaster's course. As McNulty remembered, "He wanted us (the engineers) to 'push the envelope' in our design". And push the envelope they did! Instead of a series of straightforward hills, Koch's emphasis on saving trees made them add incredible twists and turns through the forested area, saving what trees they could along the way. And by doing so, McNulty feels that Will's vision truly helped give the coaster an added edge of mystery.

The new coaster design and location were finally determined. Ground-breaking occurred in early September 1994 with construction set to begin shortly thereafter. To help save in construction

When laying out The Raven, Holiday World knew that a high-speed turnaround over Lake Rudolph had to be a part of the ride. *Holiday World photo.*

costs, much of the initial work such as installing the concrete footer supports for the coaster would be done in-house by Holiday World's own staff. So now what to name it? Enter Tim O'Brien, editor of *Amusement Business* magazine. Since it was being built in the Halloween section of the park, O'Brien suggested to Will Koch, "Why not call it 'The Raven?'" after Edgar Allan Poe's infamous poem with supernatural overtones about the descent into madness by a man who lost his love to death as a mysterious talking raven keeps reciting "Nevermore!" O'Brien's suggestion was that riders will want to ride the coaster "Evermore!" as a play on the Raven's famous catchphrase. The Kochs loved the suggestion, and the new coaster would forevermore be dubbed The Raven.

Construction of The Raven took just under nine months to complete. At just over $2 million, the coaster was the most expensive addition to the park in its history up until that time. It would feature a bright red six-car, 24-passenger train from renowned wooden roller coaster train manufacturer Philadelphia Toboggan Coasters (PTC), complete with the ride's logo featuring a sinister-looking raven behind the lettering. In a CCI press release, Denise Dinn Larrick was quoted that "It's going to be a different design of coaster for CCI. . . . This ride will have speed, it will have banking—lots of different elements from different coaster designs. It's just going to be an exceptional ride for the park."

The station resembles a gothic Victorian-era style home reminiscent of the house featured in the Alfred Hitchcock movie *Psycho* or possibly even that of the *Addams Family*. Although the actual loading platform

Memories of Will Koch and The Raven

Larry R. Bill

I first met Will Koch in late June 1994 when Holiday World was considering the addition of a wooden roller coaster. Denise Dinn-Larrick, president of Custom Coasters International (CCI), and I met with Will and his father, Bill Koch, at Holiday World. It was evident from that first meeting that Will was highly technical. He had earned a BS in electrical engineering from Notre Dame and an MS in computer science from USC. He had thoroughly researched wood coasters.

Will showed us the area of the park that he planned to use for the coaster. It was a wooded area between the main entrance to the park and a picnic pavilion near Lake Rudolph. It had a 50-foot difference in elevation from the fence line at the parking lot to the low point of the site. He wanted a ride through the woods and to remove trees only as necessary. He wanted to use the terrain to his advantage.

In the summer of 1994, CCI's design team consisted of Dennis McNulty and me. During the first week of July 1994, Dennis and I were on site at Holiday World gathering topographic data and the locations of large trees within the wooded area allotted for the new ride.

Over the next couple of months, the design progressed through numerous conceptual sketches and drawings presented to Holiday World for their consideration. Will wanted to have the station near the entrance to the park behind the children's area. He wanted people to be able to see the structure from the parking lot. Will wanted to use property near the picnic pavilion that overlooked Lake Rudolph to allow the coaster to interact with the park patrons in the pavilion. By skirting the pavilion and having the ride go out over the lake, the ride path provided that interaction while creating an exciting, picturesque turn around over water.

Coming back into the woods from Lake Rudolph provided an opportunity for a large drop into the woods and then a race through the woods, weaving among the trees. With the ride path traversing through the woods, it was necessary to accommodate the continued use of existing access roads within that part of the park and to avoid the earthen dam used for Lake Rudolph. There was also a small waterway that needed to be crossed.

The initial contract was to be for a one-train operation. However, an area parallel to the station, along the ride centerline, was set aside for a future transfer table, so the park could easily add a second train at a later date.

In mid-September 1994, Jeff Mason, construction superintendent for CCI, and I were on site at Holiday World laying out the centerline of the proposed coaster. Will

Holiday World team members pause to celebrate the completion of The Raven. *Holiday World photo.*

was a hands-on park owner committed to the park and his guests. After completing the layout, Will met with Jeff and me to walk the centerline of the proposed coaster. As part of this review, we made a few adjustments to the centerline. Considerations were given to limiting how close the ride path should get to the pavilion and to significant trees within the woods and the best place to cross the small waterway.

Working closely with Will and his vision for the park was a memorable experience for me. Although it was a hot, muggy day in southern Indiana, we were meeting with a park owner not in an office conference room, but sitting on an old fallen tree in the middle of the very woods that the coaster would travel.

The ride was later named The Raven and opened May 6, 1995.

Larry Bill, is a principal designer and engineer who helped create all three wooden roller coasters for Holiday World, first working with Custom Coasters International and then becoming a co-owner and engineer for The Gravity Group.

was built and designed by CCI, Holiday World's talented carpenters created the elaborate façade and theming. The coaster features an 80-foot-high lift hill that crests just to the left of the park's main entrance gate. The first drop at 86 feet goes below ground level next to the parking lot into a covered tunnel at the bottom. The ride then rises up, turns to the right, and then immediately goes down a second, smaller drop before approaching the much-anticipated swoop-turn over Lake Rudolph. A surprisingly large midcourse 61-foot drop into the woods comes out of nowhere thanks to the natural topography that the coaster was built on. A total height difference between the crest of the lift hill to bottom of the midcourse drop is 110 feet. The finale of the ride features a series of low-to-the-ground banked speed turns snaking through the woods giving a fast, furious finish to the 2,800 feet of track.

On the day that the final pieces of metal track were installed, excitement was building among the construction crew. After nine long months, they wanted to test the ride. According to engineer Dennis McNulty, some construction workers jumped into

The Raven's first
drop was placed
next to the front
entrance to give
guests a hint
at what was to
come. *Holiday
World photo.*

The Raven's first drop plunges riders into a 120-foot-long tunnel. *Holiday World photo.*

The Raven was designed to take maximum advantage of the natural terrain. *Holiday World photo.*

Aerial view of The Raven shows how it was carefully built through the existing trees. *Holiday World photo.*

the train even before they had a chance to test the ride. So, the first complete test runs had actual people riding the coaster, as opposed to typical sandbags. Needless to say, they knew that they had a huge hit during those first test rides!

The Raven was ready for flight for Media Day on Wednesday, May 3, 1995, where representatives of the media as well as several political dignitaries were invited to take the first rides. Will's young daughter Leah was too timid to take that first front seat ride with her father. According to former public relations director, Paula Werne, they decided to leave Leah's seat open for the ghost of Edgar Allan Poe to take that first ride with her father instead. The ride then

The Raven Fact Sheet

Opened	May 6, 1995
Design company	Custom Coasters, West Chester, Ohio
Lead designers	Larry Bill, Dennis McNulty
Concept	Will Koch
Length	2,800 feet
Lift hill height	80 feet
First drop	85 feet
Height difference	110 feet from top of lift hill to lowest point on ride
Maximum speed	48 mph
Ride time	1 minute, 30 seconds
Trains	Two 24-passenger Philadelphia Toboggan Coasters trains (six cars per train, four seats per car)
Tunnels	One
Lumber	Southern yellow pine

The crew that helped bring The Raven to life included (*from left*) Bill Koch, Scott Macdonald, Denise Dinn Larrick (both from Custom Coasters International), Will Koch, Santa Claus, Pat Koch, Lori Koch, Tom Rebbie, and Bill Dauphinee (both from Philadelphia Toboggan Coasters). *Holiday World photo.*

opened to the public on May 6 when Holiday World kicked off its 1995 season. Huge crowds stood eagerly in line to get their first rides on this new thrilling wooden coaster.

One cannot emphasize enough the overall success that Holiday World had with the opening of The Raven. Will Koch estimated that attendance would jump 18 percent during the ride's first year of operation. They never expected that the attendance for the 1995 season would actually spike to a 40 percent increase! Literally overnight, Holiday World

went from a modest local theme park to a park that was suddenly thrust into a global spotlight. Coaster enthusiasts from across the country and around the world *had* to ride what was suddenly the hottest new ride in the country. During the day, The Raven is an exciting and exhilarating trip through the woods. But at night, it takes on a completely different personality as the lack of lights and the dense trees obscure the track from sight. Like The Beast before it, it quickly became legendary as night rides became one of the most sought-after riding experiences by enthusiasts everywhere, even before the internet had truly taken off to help spread the word.

To help solidify the coaster's popularity, the park held their first *Stark Raven Mad* event on July 21, 1995, to allow select members of amusement park and roller coaster enthusiast organizations to get their first rides, including the coveted night rides, on The Raven. Over 180 attended that first of what would become an annual enthusiast event at the park, and attendance would grow each year. (The event would eventually be renamed *Holiwood Nights* to include later coaster additions that were added over the years.) And partially because of this event, The Raven jumped into the top of many polls published by various amusement-related publications and organizations such as *Inside Track* and the National Amusement Park Historical Association's annual survey. It eventually made number 1 in 2000 on one of the most prestigious amusement park polls, the *Amusement Today* Golden Ticket Awards. The Raven held onto that number 1 spot for four consecutive years through 2003. The legacy of The Raven continues to this day, ranking highly every year among wooden roller coaster enthusiasts. The American Coaster Enthusiasts (ACE) designated The Raven as an ACE Roller Coaster Landmark in 2016 due to its historic significance in successfully promoting wooden roller coaster additions for smaller to mid-size amusement parks such as Holiday World.

Holidog Gets a New Home and Free Unlimited Drinks for Everyone

With the enormous success of the Raven, Holiday World's attendance grew exponentially year after year, having record seasons of attendance for the next several seasons. During that time after the opening of The Raven, attention was given to expanding Splashin' Safari to help accommodate the ever-growing crowds. Splashin' Safari was becoming equally popular among guests and was also a major catalyst to the ever-increasing crowds as water parks had become equally big businesses for attractions across the country. The success of The Raven also allowed for the retirement of the Firecracker coaster after the 1997 season. Firecracker was a popular ride at Holiday World, but its milder thrills quickly became outdated when compared to The Raven. Firecracker was sold to Jolly Roger Amusement Park in Ocean City, Maryland, for the 1998 season and reportedly continues to operate on the fair circuits in the Midwest today.

Firecracker once held a prominent spot within the loop of the Freedom Train and Mother Goose Land, overlooking the corner of Indiana State Routes 162 and 245 (Christmas Blvd), making it quite visible from the highway. But this location would become the site of a larger project that would be more in line with the Mother Goose theme of the train ride—a whole new children's area themed to the park's popular mascot, Holidog located where the Firecracker once stood. Costing $1.2 million dollars, the new area would be known as Holidog's Funtown. Among the new area's offerings:

- Holidog's Treehouse, a three-story interactive family play structure
- Just for Pups, a smaller play area for preschoolers
- Magic Waters area with squirting fountains where children could get wet on hot days
- Holidog's All Star Theater featuring shows starring Holidog and his friends
- Holidog statue for family photo opportunities
- Hot Diggity Dogs featuring hot dogs and other fun foods for everyone

Holidog's Funtown offered Holiday World's youngest guests a second kids area themed after the beloved park mascot. *Jim Futrell photo.*

The Howler offered younger guests and their families their very own roller coaster experience. *Jim Futrell photo.*

Also included in this new area would be two new family rides from Italian manufacturer Zamperla, a family jeep ride called Doggone Trail, and a brand-new family roller coaster, The Howler. The Howler would have the distinction of its six-car train themed to look just like Holidog himself! The steel roller coaster, suitable for kids over 36 inches tall with their parents, takes riders up a 13-foot lift to allow smaller thrill seekers a chance to enjoy milder thrills with Holidog along 262.5 feet of track. Another Zamperla family ride, Kitty's Tea Party, would be added to the area in 2013.

A major milestone decision announced in the fall of 1999 would have much more impact on attendance, creating quite a stir in the amusement industry that would premiere during the 2000 season. After careful consideration and calculation, Holiday World made the bold move to offer free unlimited soft drinks for all guests. Since soft drink sales are typically a big source of revenue for most other businesses, the move was unprecedented. However, the promotion paid off as positive word of mouth soon permeated the market, helping to bump attendance. In later years, the park would also promote free sunscreen and free inner tubes along with the unlimited soft drinks as part of admission to the park. Of course, free parking has always been offered since the park began as Santa Claus Land in 1946.

A New Legend Emerges

The huge success of The Raven had Will Koch wanting bigger thrills for Holiday World. While attending No Coaster Con in Chicago in January 1999, a midwinter event held by ACE every January to allow park representatives to talk about what's new at their parks, Will Koch came armed with several concept drawings of a possible new coaster addition for the park. Surprising everyone in attendance, he showed the upcoming plans for the possible new coaster. However, he wanted feedback from the "experts," namely, the coaster enthusiasts attending the event. No contracts had been submitted or signed yet with any construction company, but he told attendees that he was very pleased with what CCI had done with creating The Raven. He also wanted possible name suggestions for the new ride. Approximately fifty-eight formal suggestions were submitted to Holiday World suggesting what they'd like to see in a new wood coaster for the park. They also received about sixty name suggestions from attendees for the possible new ride. Surprisingly, nothing unusual or unrealistic was submitted by those who participated. Most participants wanted more "airtime" (out-of-your-seat thrills) while others suggested more lateral forces from tight turns or helixes. Will also utilized the fledgling internet, soliciting ideas on enthusiasts' forums for more design suggestions. In all, he received more than two hundred replies with some great input into how to make the coaster even better.

Will was quite pleased with their submissions and finally met with CCI representatives later that month to decide what the new coaster would consist of. It was decided that the new ride would also be built in the Halloween section of the park through the heavily wooded terrain beyond the Frightful Falls log flume. It would also be much larger, faster, and a more aggressive ride than The Raven complete with more drops, more turns, and would also include a tunneled double helix, another nod to Will's favorite non-Holiday World coaster, The Beast.

On June 16, 1999, Holiday World officially announced their newest wooden roller coaster addition that would open in 2000. The Legend, based on the Washington Irving story "The Legend of Sleepy Hollow," riders would get a chance to experience the hapless schoolteacher Ichabod Crane's frightening chase through the woods by the relentless Headless

While most of The Legend was designed to travel through the woods, the park wanted to make sure it interacted with existing park attractions and had it travel through Frightful Falls right up to the midway. *Holiday World photo.*

Like its older brother, The Legend was built to take advantage of the park's trees. *Holiday World photo.*

Cruising Toward an Oasis

How Free Unlimited Soft Drinks Came to Holiday World

Mike Johannes began working for Holiday World on October 22, 1992. Little did he know that October 22 was also the birthday of Will Koch, president and CEO of Holiday World. As the new director of sales for the park, one of Mike's many duties was to oversee group sales for the park and try to make sure that each group was satisfied with their outing to Holiday World. He would work together with what was known unofficially within park management as "the marketing council," which consisted of three people, John Chidester, director of marketing, Paula Werne, director of communications and public relations, and himself.

When a group would book a pavilion and catered meal in the park, unlimited soft drinks would be included at an additional cost with the meal at the pavilion and offered only in the pavilion. Shortly after starting his position, Mike suggested that they use colored wristbands to identify those attending group functions to allow them to receive drinks from any refreshment area in the park. Needless to say, that the concept was very well received by the guests.

In the fall of 1993 after the park had closed for the season, Mike and his wife took a Caribbean cruise with Will and Lori Koch. While on the cruise, Mike marveled at the way all food was included in the price of the cruise ticket, but with the exception of water, all drinks including soft drinks were not included. He then suggested to Will that he felt that Holiday World could do that better for their guests by selling an unlimited drink plan.

During the course of the next year, the marketing council tried to figure out how many drinks an average person would consume in a day. Surprisingly, they found out that an average guest consumed about 2.7 drinks in an average day at the park. Guests who were not with group outings began noticing the wristbands and questioned how they could buy one too. So the marketing council began to include drinks as additional charges to consignment tickets that would be sold by third-party venues such as banks, churches, schools, etc. The drink vouchers became so popular that lines at the refreshment stands were getting much longer as people wanting unlimited drinks interfered with those also in line for food. The solution was to set up portable soft drink stations at various points around the park.

Finally, in the fall of 1999, the marketing council suggested to Will Koch the possibility of adding free unlimited drinks for all tickets since more than half of the tickets sold were also paying the upcharge for unlimited drinks. With a new coaster opening in 2000 (The Legend), they figured that if they upped the daily ticket cost by $4.00, they could make this work. When Will Koch announced this plan at the annual IAAPA trade show in November 1999, others in the amusement industry told him he was crazy to do so, as soft drink sales usually represented a major source of revenue for most other amusement and theme parks. But Will, having made an executive decision, pushed along the concept of offering "free unlimited drinks" to all guests for the 2000

The Legend became a new anchor in Halloween, towering over Frightful Falls. *Jim Futrell photo.*

season. And it certainly made a lasting impact on attendance and marketability. Consumer response was overwhelmingly positive and attendance shot up dramatically. They used the "free unlimited drinks" promotion in all of their advertising for the season, which gave Holiday World another record year in attendance.

They built the first "Pepsi Oasis" across from The Legend station, with three more added in other locations during the season. A few more Oasis stands were constructed in later expansion projects, and today, "free unlimited drinks" is synonymous with a day's outing to Holiday World. The following November at the 2000 IAAPA trade show, Holiday World was honored with the "Best Promotion Award" for their Free Unlimited Soft Drink Promotion during the trade show's closing ceremonies.

Mike Johannes likes to boast that when Will Koch found out that he hired him on his birthday, he told Mike that he "was one of the best birthday presents that he ever received!"

Horseman at the climax of that famous story. Construction began several months earlier before the park had opened to the public and was well underway when the announcement was made. The Legend of Sleepy Hollow was also the most suggested name or theme to be used for the ride by the enthusiasts polled. It was decided to shorten the name to The Legend, with a sinister shadow of the Headless Horseman as the ride's logo. According to sources at the park and engineers that worked with Will Koch on the design, the goal was to possibly create the best coaster operating that could defeat even The Raven in the rankings.

CCI was chosen once again to design and build the new coaster. CCI engineers Larry Bill, Jeff Mason, and Dennis McNulty were among the team to help design the ride while construction supervision was overseen by foreman David Moore. The coaster would reach a maximum height of 111 feet at the top of the lift hill but had a larger first drop of 113 feet due to the slope of the hillside on which it was built.

Guests board the coaster in a recreation of a New England–style one-room schoolhouse, complete with

The Legend's swooping first drop in to the woods, seen here from Splashin' Safari, was one of its most distinctive features. *Jim Futrell photo.*

bell tower and a large chalkboard along the station's one wall. A single six-car, twenty-four-passenger purple train from Gerstlauer Amusement Rides, a German ride manufacturer, was used for The Legend for its first two seasons as CCI was utilizing these types of trains for new ride developments at the time. As the train leaves the station, the school bell is rung by the ride operators. After riders ascend the large lift hill, they make an almost full U-turn to the first leftward diving swoop drop through the first of five tunnels. Just before descending, riders hear a recorded wolf howl to add to the terror. Then riders experience a series of airtime-producing speed hills while paralleling the water park of Splashin' Safari.

The Legend and the Tree

**Chad Miller, Engineer and Principal,
The Gravity Group**

I had been at Custom Coasters for only a couple of years when we started working on the design for Holiday World's second wooden coaster, The Legend. Larry Bill and Dennis McNulty had been the ones primarily working on the design. But CCI was in the midst of designing seven coasters for the 2000 seasons, and so even as the low engineer on the totem pole, I was afforded the opportunity to get more involved with design than I might have otherwise been. I wanted to try some "new math" to generate some coaster geometry in a way that was outside what CCI had been doing previously. There were no systems or programs in place to do this, so it was a slow and tedious process. Once I had created a small section of the ride path using this method, it was difficult to make adjustments without having to repeat the whole cumbersome process.

So, let's back up a little bit. Earlier in the ride design process, Holiday World had gone to the trouble of identifying several large trees on the coaster site that they wanted to avoid cutting down, similar to what they had done for the Raven five years earlier. While attempts were made to have the ride miss as many of these trees as possible, there was one that we just couldn't seem to avoid.

This is where my "new math" came in. By doing things a little differently, we were able to miss this tree, and at the same time, implement what we felt like was a pretty cool new addition to our coaster design toolbox. But as mentioned earlier, this was a long and tedious process to get it just right and still miss the tree.

Fast forward a few months and Holiday World is clearing the site for construction, except for the valuable trees, which had been marked to identify them as ones that were not to be cut down. Unfortunately, we received a phone call from the job site informing us that the tree . . . THE TREE . . . had accidentally been cut down. So, while that particular section of the ride had been painstakingly reworked and modified to save a large old tree that was ultimately cut down, not all was lost. The implementation of our new design tool on The Legend was the beginning of what eventually evolved into something that we made more efficient use of on many of CCI's rides after that and was the precursor to the mathematical process we use today at The Gravity Group. I like to think of that tree as a martyr for the future of wooden coaster design.

The Legend Fact Sheet

Opened   May 6, 2000

Design company   Custom Coasters International, West Chester, Ohio

Lead designers   Larry Bill, Dennis McNulty

Concept   Will Koch

Length   4,042 feet

Lift hill height   111 feet

First drop   113 feet

Height difference   116 feet from top of lift hill to lowest point on ride

Maximum speed   59 mph

Ride time   2 minutes

Trains   Two 24-passenger Philadelphia Toboggan Coasters trains (six cars per train, four seats per car)

Tunnels   Five, including one underground tunnel

Lumber   Southern yellow pine

Riders celebrate the opening of the Legend.
Holiday World photo.

Another swooping drop sends the train careening back along this fairly straight out-and-back section of the ride that features the ride's second, partially underground tunnel until it bears to the right and enters the double-tunneled helix, causing intense lateral sensations as the train rises and drops along the right-turning middle section of the ride. A few more drops and heavily banked turns then have the train diving down under the lift hill for Frightful Falls (which became a covered bridge in 2016 to signify the final encounter that Ichabod Crane had with the Headless Horseman in the story). During this section of the ride, a recorded "Don't look back!" can be heard as if the Headless Horseman were right behind the riders. One last drop to the left and a quick 180-degree banked turnaround, and the train returns to the schoolhouse station.

The Legend became another instant classic for Holiday World, with another record-breaking season with attendance for 2000. Members of ACE held their twenty-third annual convention at Holiday World in June of 2000 and, needless to say, were not disappointed with the park's two magnificent wooden creations. Many of the attendees were voters for the *Amusement Today* Golden Ticket Awards. Will Koch's goal was to make the new coaster better than Raven and was hoping to achieve the status of "Best Wooden Coaster" with The Legend that year. And Holiday World did achieve that goal for 2000, but ironically not with The Legend, but with The Raven as the then five-year-old wooden coaster shot to the top of the rankings for four consecutive years through 2003. This was a true testament to the greatness that CCI created with The Raven. However, The Legend was no slouch either as it debuted in the number seven

"Don't Look Back!"

Korey Kiepert and Mike Graham were newly hired engineers as Custom Coasters International was working on The Legend at Holiday World in 2000. Once the wooden coaster was completed and had opened to the public, they were brought in to help tweak it to make the train go faster, as it wasn't going as fast as originally designed. The train, purchased from Gerstlauer Amusement Rides of Germany, had some speed issues due to the way that the bearings on the wheel assemblies were designed.

Korey and Mike were assigned to help make the train operate faster, but to do so meant that they would have to work on the coaster after the park had closed for the day. Both engineers recall that this process resulted in them being covered in axle grease from head to toe as they tried to lubricate the wheel assemblies to help reduce friction. They were left completely alone in the park with just the lights on in the immediate area of The Legend's station where they were working. Both men recalled how creepy the feeling was that they were the only two in the park that night. No sounds of laughter or screams, no music playing from the park's sound systems.

They would hear just the sounds of the natural surroundings of the area except when they occasionally dispatched the train for testing. Unexpectedly in the middle of the night, they were startled by a loud, "Don't look back!" They looked around and at each other, wondering who had said it, but they saw no one. A few moments later, they heard "Don't look back!" again! They then realized it was a recorded spiel that played when the train returned to the station. However, no train had been dispatched. Something had triggered the sensor to play the sound, possibly even their own unwitting actions. Regardless of how it was triggered, it was certainly a startling experience for both of them!

spot in the Best Wooden Coaster category that debut year. It shot up to number five in 2001 and 2003, peaking at number four in 2002. As with The Raven, The Legend continues to rank highly among roller coaster lovers today. A transfer track and two brand new wooden coaster trains from PTC were added to The Legend in 2002 to increase capacity as attendance continued to climb for the park. The Gerstlauer train was sold to Six Flags Worlds of Adventure (the former Geauga Lake) in Aurora, Ohio where it was used on their Raging Wolf Bobs coaster until the park closed permanently at the end of the 2007 season.

And the Awards Go To . . .

Although the *Amusement Today* Golden Ticket award for Best Wooden Coaster was certainly an achievement to be proud of for the park, there were several other Golden Ticket awards that Holiday World had much more long-lasting success with over the years. From 1998 through 2011 (excluding 2009), Holiday World was granted the Friendliest Park award by Golden Ticket voters. Beginning in 2000 through today, Holiday World has the distinct honor of being the Cleanest Park. This honor is no small feat and can be traced directly to Pat Koch, Bill Koch's wife. Lovingly called the "Queen of Clean" by many of the park's staff, she is the true matriarch of the Koch family's legacy. Pat's spotless attention to cleanliness has been adopted by the entire staff of the park, where everyone takes great pride in keeping the status of Cleanest Park in the amusement industry. Newer employees learn right away that "If you have time enough to lean, you have time enough to clean". A policy that is still very much in use to this day!

Unfortunately, the tragic events of the terrorist attacks on September 11, 2001, brought a dark time to the nation and changed the world forever. Just six days later, Holiday World and the Koch family

Will Koch accepting the Golden Ticket Award for cleanest park in 2007, one of dozens of awards the park has won. Amusement Today *photo.*

suffered their own personal loss with the death of Bill Koch at the age of 86. Not only did the park lose the patriarch who guided the transition of his father Louis's vision of the quaint Santa Claus Land into what is now Holiday World, but the Koch family lost their father, grandfather, and for Pat Koch, her beloved husband of 41 years. His leadership and guidance were felt everywhere, not only in the park but in the entire town of Santa Claus and the surrounding region. He was also a great mentor for not only his children Will, Dan, Kristi, Philip, and Natalie, but for everyone involved in the operations and development of the park, as well as the town. Thankfully, his legacy for the park and the region is secure and thriving and should live on for many, many more years to come.

ZOOMbabwe, the world's largest enclosed water slide was added to Splashin' Safari in 2003 while a few

Hallow Swings, a custom designed Flying Carousel ride replaced the Banshee in 2003. *Holiday World photo.*

Liberty Launch, an S & S Power Double Shot tower replaced the Hall of Famous Americans in 2003. *Jim Futrell photo.*

removals occurred to make way for newer attractions. The Frontier Farm would close after the 2001 season, while in 2002 one of the park's most popular attractions, Banshee, a Chance Falling Star ride that opened in 1986, came to the end of its service life and needed to be removed. When the news reached Will's daughters Leah and Lauren, both sisters begged their father Will to keep the ride as it was one of their favorites. Unfortunately, their pleas were in vain as it would cost too much to refurbish. Instead, for the 2003 season, Holiday World would feature not one, but two new rides.

Replacing Banshee would be a flying carousel swing ride from Zamperla. Called HallowSwings, the new spinning swing ride was custom designed for the Halloween section of the park. The colorful canopy is adorned with whimsical images of jack-o'-lanterns, scarecrows, witches, skeletons, and other playful Halloween figures, while the central column features children wearing Halloween costumes. The ride rises to a height of 40 feet and undulates while the swings with riders stretch outward during the ride's cycle. Will Koch was quoted in a park press release that "HallowSwings is a work of art—and a real crowd-pleaser."

The second new ride of 2003 was Liberty Launch, a Double Shot tower ride from S & S Power (now S & S Sansei). Built in the 4th of July section of the park, riders are shot 80 feet up the tower via compressed air, and then are shot back down the tower giving a tremendous free-fall sensation. The entire thrilling cycle is repeated once again. Liberty Launch took the place of the Hall of Famous Americans, which was retired after fifty seasons.

Including the new Zinga family water slide addition to Splashin' Safari, the park spent $3.8 million in improvements for the 2003 season thanks to steadily increasing crowds to the park. It was the largest non–roller coaster investment in the park's history at that point.

Holiday World continued to upgrade its attractions line up in 2005 when the Roundhouse was retired and replaced by the Revolution. *Jim Futrell photo.*

Although 2004 saw the addition of the popular Jungle Racer mat racer water slide for Splashin' Safari, a more prestigious honor was bestowed on Holiday World in November during the annual International Association of Amusement Parks and Attractions (IAAPA) tradeshow in Orlando, Florida. The amusement industry's most coveted award, the Applause Award, cosponsored by Liseberg Park in Sweden and *Amusement Business,* a trade journal, announced that Holiday World and Splashin' Safari would be the 2004-2005 recipient of the prestigious international honor. Among the criteria to be considered for the award include "foresight, originality, and creativity, plus sound business development and profitability" according to the press release. At the time, Holiday World was the only American finalist that year, along with two distinguished European amusement parks, Gardaland in Verona, Italy, and Tivoli Gardens in Copenhagen, Denmark. At that time, Holiday World was the smallest park ever to win the award. Previous US-based parks that won the award included Cedar Point in Sandusky, Ohio; Universal Studios Florida in Orlando; and Disneyland in Anaheim, California. A large replica of the award featuring two hands clapping was installed in the fountain just inside the park's main entrance in 2005. The replica award was retired from public view in 2019 but was relocated to the employee entrance as a testament to all of the employees who helped to make the recognition possible.

New for 2005 was an updated version of the popular Round Up ride called Revolution that was added to the 4th of July section, replacing the park's original Round Up ride known as the Roundhouse. The Sellner Tilt-a-Whirl called the Virginia Reel (that was also once known as Wynken', Blynken', and Nod during its Santa Claus Land days) would also be retired that season. Also new for 2005, a new wave pool called Bahari Wave would nearly double the size of Splashin' Safari. But these additions were just a precursor to what was to come in 2006. The largest addition in the park's history was about to make waves in 2006, including a whole new holiday to explore.

Pilgrimage to a New Holiday Leads to Even Greater Heights

Flashback to September 2002. Will Koch invited several former Custom Coasters International engineers who had just formed a new wooden roller coaster design company called The Gravity Group, to the park. CCI, which had designed both The Raven and The Legend for Holiday World, had fallen on hard times in early 2002, and the business closed, leaving their talented ride designers and engineers suddenly unemployed. Among those invited to the park that day were Larry Bill, president and co-owner of the newly formed company, The Gravity Group (GG), who was also one of the key designers for both of the previous Holiday World coasters. Their main reason for the visit was to create a proposal for a transfer track and block brake system on The Raven as Will Koch wanted to bring much-needed and long-overdue two-train operations to his original coaster. According to GG engineer Korey Kiepert, Will also wanted to reveal something else, a much larger long-term project. After discussing their concepts for the new transfer track on The Raven, Will took the group to the top of the ZOOMbabwe water slide tower. While pointing to the heavily wooded sloping hillside on the north end of the property, he began to describe how he wanted a gigantic out-and-back wooden roller coaster. A photo was taken with the crew of the proposed site showing nothing but trees and undeveloped property. A few years later in the fall of 2004, GG engineers Larry Bill and Chad Miller returned with other staff to the park on a rainy, dreary day to hear Will Koch's detailed views of what he wanted with his new coaster. It would also be the anchor for a new, yet-to-be-named themed holiday area of the park, the first to be added to the park since 1984 when Santa Claus Land became Holiday World. The massive new coaster would be visible from Highway 162 and would help to redefine the skyline of the park once again.

As with all roller coaster designs, several different iterations of the ride were drawn up—most of which followed a linear out-and-back layout. Will Koch wanted more turns, something more than to turn the train around. He also wanted three massive hills on the outward leg, all with drops of more than one hundred feet. And he wanted an abundance

Will Koch worked with The Gravity Group to design a wooden roller coaster like no other. *The Gravity Group image.*

of tunnels. Koch literally wanted to build the best wooden roller coaster in the world. Finally, he didn't want just a set of smaller hills returning the train straight back to the station but more serpentine action that would cut back and forth through the main structure of the ride. Some of GG engineers dubbed this final section of the ride the "Ewok Adventure," named after the speeder bike scene from the 1983 Star Wars film, *Return of the Jedi*. This portion zigzags through the trees and structure with low-to-the-ground banked turns, some reaching close to 90 degrees.

After a final design was chosen, Will Koch contacted Larry Bill who was working on another coaster project (Hades at Mt. Olympus theme park in Wisconsin Dells, Wisconsin). Land clearing began in March 2005 with construction commencing soon after. Unlike the previous two coasters for Holiday World, this new ride would be built with a steel structure, but with wooden track beds. It would still be classified as a wooden coaster even with nearly all of the structure being built with galvanized steel.

On July 13, 2005, the park made a formal announcement introducing the new ride as well as the new holiday-themed area that it would anchor. Thanksgiving would become the fourth holiday represented in the park, and the new coaster would be themed to the Pilgrims' expedition aboard the *Mayflower* during their journey across the Atlantic Ocean to the New World. The massive new wooden coaster would be named The Voyage and feature a 159-foot-tall lift hill, with three consecutive drops over 100 feet each, the first being at 154 feet, the second at 107 feet, and the third just over 100 feet with a below-ground tunnel. In fact, there was a total of five underground tunnels (a record!) including one underground tunnel with a triple down dip! It also included two aboveground tunnels as part of the incredibly large layout that is an amazing 6,442 feet long. Engineer Korey Kiepert remembers originally

The Voyage Fact Sheet

Opened   May 6, 2006

Design company The Gravity Group, Cincinnati, Ohio

Lead designers Larry Bill, Michael Graham, Chad Miller, Korey Kiepert

Concept   Will Koch

Length   6,442 feet (1.2 miles), currently second longest in the world

Lift hill height 159 feet

Major drops   1st hill, 154 feet; 2nd hill, 107 feet; 3rd hill, 100 feet

Maximum speed   67.4 mph

Ride time   2 minutes, 45 seconds

Trains   Two 24-passenger Philadelphia Toboggan Coasters trains (six cars per train, four seats per car)

Tunnels   Eight including five underground tunnels

Lumber   320,000 estimated board feet of Southern yellow pine

Steel   750 estimated tons

The Voyage was the tallest structure ever constructed at Holiday World. It towered over the new Thanksgiving area and the rest of the park. *Holiday World photo.*

trying to theme the station as the *Mayflower* itself, but it was decided that the loading area would resemble a Pilgrim-era New England structure instead.

The design of The Voyage was a group effort by everyone at The Gravity Group but included GG's four principal engineers and owners: Larry Bill, Michael Graham, Chad Miller, and Korey Kiepert. Their combined talent along with Will Koch's creative input helped to form The Voyage's unique blend of thrills and excitement. Everyone at GG had a task to do. Everyone played a part in its final realization. It was a massive effort by a talented group of people. In the end, they all helped to realize Will Koch's grand vision of the ride. The ride was engineered by GG, and the actual construction of the coaster was done in-house by Holiday World.

After 13 long months, it was almost time to test the new ride. Sean Strahl, maintenance planner and lead caretaker for all of the wooden coasters at Holiday World, remembers the first test runs. Initially, there were three seven-car, twenty-eight-passenger trains built by PTC for The Voyage, but after a few seasons it was determined that only two six-car trains were needed to run the coaster efficiently and safely.

When testing time came, instead of using sandbags or water dummies for the first few test runs, the park used what was easily available in the cornfields of southern Indiana—100-pound sacks of corn. The coaster performed flawlessly with its corn-filled sacks traversing the course. But The Voyage is an intense and relentless ride. And the sacks containing the corn weren't as sturdy as first thought, as thousands of kernels of corn were flung all around the ride throughout its long course. This resulted in an unexpected "crop" of cornstalks growing around and through the ride structure over the course of the ride's first summer! Strahl remembers seeing corn growing from just about anywhere around the ride that year and later revealed that they had

Above, A series of 90-degree turns are one of The Voyage's many distinctive features. *Holiday World photo.*

Facing, The first three 100-foot-plus hills of The Voyage make it a skyline-defining ride. *Holiday World photo.*

this same unique problem when testing all of their wooden coasters: a new "crop" appeared around each coaster's structure. The Voyage just had more of it due to its large size. They also had an issue of the corn decomposing in the underground tunnels causing a rather unpleasant smell, which was quickly cleaned up before the ride opened to the public.

On May 6, 2006, as part of Holiday World's sixtieth anniversary, The Voyage and the new Thanksgiving section of the park would open to the public. Costing over $6.5 million, it was easily the largest and most expensive addition to the park in its history. Koch once again was aiming for the best wooden coaster experience, and this time he succeeded as The Voyage

A portion of The Voyage's structure was utilized as the entrance portal for the new Thanksgiving area. *Jim Futrell photo.*

took "Best New Attraction" for the 2006 season in the *Amusement Today* Golden Ticket Awards. It then became the number-one wooden coaster for five consecutive years, from 2007 through 2011, continuing to place in the top five ever since. During the "Holiwood Nights" event that first year, Tony Perkins, Holiday World's director of maintenance, recalls that stormy weather was off in the distance that evening. Usually, the park would shut down the larger rides due to the threat of lightning in the area. Will Koch asked to keep the ride running as long as safely possible to give attendees the best experience

ever. Tony said, "It was an eerie, almost spiritual experience" riding that coaster with distant lightning flashing in the night sky. A new roller coaster legend set sail that year with The Voyage. Will Koch summed it up best, words that The Gravity Group likes to use in their advertising, "I think that The Voyage is a ride that will stand the test of time and be long remembered as one of the great achievements in our industry."

As immense in size as The Voyage was, it was only one part of the massive new Thanksgiving expansion area for Holiday World. The other major ride addition

Located across the midway from The Voyage, Gobbler Getaway was Holiday World's first dark ride. *Jim Futrell photo.*

for the Thanksgiving expansion was Gobbler Getaway, a lighthearted, interactive dark ride from Sally Corporation of Jacksonville, Florida. Housed in an 8,732-square-foot building, the attraction takes visitors back in time approximately two hundred years to the town of Autumn Falls where vibrant autumn colors last all year long. Guests in the queue area encounter the animatronic character of Aunt Abigail Van Snoodle, who tells the story of that fateful day in 1775 when all of Farmer Van Snoodle's turkeys disappeared just before Thanksgiving. She explains that the turkeys will answer only to the special turkey callers that the townsfolk use to help round up the missing fowls. Guests then board the specialized Turkey Trotter vehicles designed by Italian ride manufacturer, Bertazzon. Each vehicle is equipped not with a "gun" but with the turkey callers that Aunt Abigail was describing, complete with electronic scoring. They are then whisked back in time to 1785 to help round up the missing turkeys in a very whimsical, often comedic, musical adventure. Guests encounter various scenes throughout the town of Autumn Falls, including the surrounding farms and countryside, where they shoot at targets to help the

Aunt Abigail Van Snoodle acts as your host on Gobbler Getaway. *Jim Futrell photo.*

interactive turkeys appear. The ride culminates with a hilarious Busby Berkeley musical finale starring all the turkeys performing in an elaborate chorus line finale. At the end of the ride, Farmer Van Snoodle doesn't have the heart to have them as Thanksgiving dinner any longer. Rather, he invites the turkeys to be his guests as he prepares an unexpected Thanksgiving meal that's sure to surprise everyone, including the turkeys! In a press release, Sally CEO John Wood felt that Gobbler Getaway was "Destined to be a classic custom attraction. . . . Not only fun for the patrons, but it is unique as it can only be found at Holiday World."

As if a whole new land, massive new roller coaster, and an elaborate dark ride weren't enough, Splashin' Safari also received its own large new addition with Bahari River, an action river attraction. The entire cost of all new additions to the park in 2006 totaled over $13.5 million and was the largest expansion ever for the park under Will Koch's leadership. The additions were enough to catapult Holiday World to new heights and the park drew over one million guests for the first time ever.

For 2007, the park continued to expand the Thanksgiving section with the addition of Turkey Whirl, a modern new version of the classic Tilt-A-

Added in 2007, Turkey Whirl was a new Tilt-A-Whirl ride with a unique twist. *Jim Futrell photo.*

Whirl from Sellner. Instead of the traditional half-domed canopy cars that Tilt-A-Whirls are famous for, the vehicles are shaped like cartoonish turkeys instead. The turkey vehicles are real crowd pleasers, especially for the kids. Also new was Plymouth Rock Café, a new cafeteria-style eating establishment added in the Thanksgiving section that specializes in full-course turkey dinners, including all of the trimmings—stuffing, mashed potatoes, and cranberry sauce among its many offerings.

A new carousel from Chance Rides was added to the 4th of July section in 2008, replacing the Thunder Bumpers bumper boat attraction. It was christened the Star Spangled Carousel, helping to give an increased patriotic atmosphere to the area. Also new that season was a 30-foot-tall family drop tower from Moser Rides called Reindeer Games that replaced the Kid's Castle play area in Rudolph's Reindeer Ranch. To round out the 2008 additions, a new children's water play structure including kid-sized slides and their own tipping bucket was added to Splashin' Safari.

The world's tallest water flume was added to the Thanksgiving section in 2009. Initially called Pilgrim's Plunge, the $4.3-million water attraction from Intamin of Switzerland boasted the world's

Will and William Koch try out the one-of-a-kind turkey-shaped cars on Turkey Whirl. *Holiday World photo.*

The Star Spangled Carousel gave Holiday World a full-sized classic carousel. *Holiday World photo.*

largest flume drop at 131 feet. Utilizing a unique split elevator system, the boats would be lifted to the top of the massive tower, then plunge downward at a 45-degree angle at speeds reaching more than 50 mph, creating a powerful wave as it hit the splash pool. Geysers would then shoot at the already soaked riders as they returned to the loading platform. The unique nature of the very wet ride allowed patrons from nearby Splashin' Safari to ride in their swimsuits or allowed those in Thanksgiving to ride with their street clothes. It was also the only attraction in Holiday World to be "moved" from one land to another without physically moving. In 2013, the ride was renamed Giraffica, technically moving from the Thanksgiving area to Splashin' Safari simply by shifting boundaries for the water park. Unfortunately, due to some operational issues with

the ride, it would close permanently at the end of the 2013 season.

In the more than two decades that Will Koch was in charge of Holiday World, the park would see the largest expansion era in its history, up until that point. The addition of Splashin' Safari, three world-class, highly ranked wooden roller coasters, and a new themed holiday section were amazing accomplishments, to be sure. His legacy was secure after taking his father Bill's place as the visionary for the park's future, which certainly looked bright under his control. Unfortunately, no one could foresee the sudden tragedy and uncertainties that the park would soon face just one year later. Thankfully, Holiday World continued to endure, and the Koch legacy carries on.

When Pilgrim's Plunge opened in 2009, it featured the world's largest flume drop. *Holiday World photo.*

Aerial view of the original Splashin' Safari shows its first two water slides and Congo River. *Holiday World photo.*

Making A Splash

How Holiday World's Splashin' Safari Became a World-Class Attraction

Ron Gustafson

When Will Koch Jr. packed the family up for late summer vacations, the road trips generally included stops at a number of amusement parks along the way.

"Will had been watching all of the other parks that were adding water parks," wife, Lori, said of her late husband's curiosity in how traditional amusement facilities, similar to Holiday World, were branching out with the addition of water attractions. "One year we loaded up the kids and did four or five parks. We had finished our daily operations (late August), but other parks were still open."

Though the Koch family's theme park had incorporated water attractions into its ride arsenal—Frightful Falls log flume (1984) and Raging Rapids raft ride (1990)—Will, then the park's president and general manager, had his sights set on taking the property to the next level by developing a full-fledged water park.

During those vacation trips three decades ago, Will specifically targeted stopovers to parks in Pennsylvania and Ohio that had some water elements in operation. Returning home, the family would quickly develop the pictures taken during their adventure and—much to Lori's surprise—there were more pictures of water parks than there were of their three children.

"I asked Will, 'Are there any pictures of the kids in here?' He thumbed through them, and said 'Yes, here they are,'" she recalled.

But the deciding factor in Holiday World's decision to dive into the water park business came after a trip to northwestern Pennsylvania.

"We went to Waldameer (Erie, Pa.) to check it out, and it was going gangbusters for them," Lori Koch said of the tour of the Water World (water park) section of the property.

Waldameer, founded in 1896, is a traditional amusement park overlooking Lake Erie and today is owned and operated by the Nelson and Gorman families. The water park opened in 1986 and, thanks to its success, has gone through numerous expansions since its inception.

"It piqued our interest, and I recall Will saying it (adding a water park) was something that would increase our attendance," she added.

Starting Up and Branding

The northern section of Holiday World's property was not developed at the time, and the Kochs saw it as the ideal location to break ground for water attractions, with 1993 earmarked as an opening.

Chronology of Splashin' Safari at Holiday World

1993
Splashin' Safari water park premiers, including the Congo River, Crocodile Isle, and the AmaZOOM and Bamboo Chute water slides

1994
The Wave pool added to Splashin' Safari

1998
Monsoon Lagoon interactive water play area added to Splashin' Safari

2002
ZOOMbabwe, the World's Largest Enclosed Water slide, opens in Splashin' Safari, which begins offering free sunscreen to all guests

2003
Huge new family water ride, Zinga, is added to Splashin' Safari; voted World's #1 Water Park Ride

2004
Jungle Racer—a 10-slide complex—and Jungle Jets are added to Splashin' Safari. Both parks are now nonsmoking. Holiday World & Splashin' Safari win the Applause Award, the smallest park ever to win the prestigious industry honor.

2005
Bahari wave pool added, beginning expansion project to double the size of Splashin' Safari

2006
Park's 60th Anniversary Season includes the addition of Bahari River to Splashin' Safari. The attraction has stronger currents than Congo River. Park's seasonal attendance tops one million guests for the first time

2007
Seven-story Bakuli (bowl in Swahili) water slide added to Splashin' Safari

2008
Kima Bay, a four-story monkey-themed waterplay attraction with seven water slides and more than 100 water play elements added to Splashin' Safari

2010
Wildebeest, the world's longest water coaster, utilizes linear induction motor technology to propel four-person boats up hills and through tunnels. Wildebeest was named the World's #1 Water Park Ride and Best New Water Park Ride in the 2010 Golden Ticket Awards, presented by industry publication *Amusement Today*

2011
Safari Sam's SplashLand, with eight water slides and loads of water-play elements for smaller children added

2012
Mammoth, the world's longest water coaster, opens in Splashin' Safari, which is named the #1 Water Park in the Nation by TripAdvisor.com

Congo River was a family favorite from the beginning. *Holiday World photo.*

2013

Hyena Falls, an in-the-dark water slide complex, opens in Splashin' Safari. Newspaper *USA Today* ranks Splashin' Safari the best water park in the nation

2017

Mammoth is certified as the World's Longest Water Coaster in the 2017 *Guinness Book of World Records*

2018

Smaller children are the focus of the elephant-themed addition, Tembo Falls junior water slides and Tembo Tides junior wave pool

2019

USA Today names Splashin' Safari the top water park in the nation, and TripAdvisor inducts Holiday World & Splashin' Safari into its Hall of Fame

2020

Cheetah Chase: The World's First Launched Water Coaster opens July 4 due to opening delays from COVID-19. Cheetah Chase is voted one of the top new amusement park attractions of 2020 by *USA Today*

As for naming the water park, a lot of potential names were brought up at directors' meetings, but no hard decision was made.

The Koch family had piled back into the car for a leisurely afternoon drive when Lori came up with another branding idea—one that would hit home in what Holiday World wanted to accomplish.

"We were all in the car and the song 'Surfin' Safari' by the Beach Boys came to mind," Lori Koch recalled. "So, I threw out the name Splashin' Safari and it took."

Lori Koch made her case with the rest of the family by pointing out that Europeans go on "holiday," otherwise known in the United States as vacation.

"If you were going on a safari, it could be said you were taking a holiday, so I said, 'Why not?' At the time we were trying to stay away from all of the other water park names and themes that were popping up—we needed something that worked for us," she contended. "We knew it would end up being Holiday World and something, we just didn't know what."

According to park records, the Koch family decided to invest $3 million over five years to get its feet wet

Splashin' Safari's smallest guests could enjoy Crocodile Isle and the Croc slide. *Holiday World photo.*

in the water park business. Splashin' Safari made its debut for the summer of '93 as planned and included four attractions for young and old.

The most popular of the offerings was Congo River, a high-capacity lazy river with single-rider tubes issued when guests entered. One of its highlights was a giant mushroom waterfall near the halfway mark of the 750-foot zigzag layout. The river also had three pedestrian bridges with rain curtains.

Crocodile Isle was a children's splash area with two pools, totaling 2,800 square feet, on two different levels. The pools, with depths averaging 12 inches, were connected by two gentle waterslides that dropped to the lower level. The low-impact play area included foam animals youngsters could slide off of as well as spray jets and a bubbling fountain.

Not to ignore thrill seekers, the park built two large serpentine tube slides that dropped from

Early view of Splashin' Safari showing all three of its original attractions. *Holiday World photo.*

Santa shows off Splashin' Safari's new for 1994 attraction—the Wave, a 21,000-square-foot wave pool. *Holiday World photo.*

a single tower and named them AmaZOOM and Bamboo Chute, keeping with the safari theme.

AmaZOOM was an enclosed attraction running 296 feet in length, while Bamboo Chute had an open run of 344 feet. Though AmaZOOM was enclosed, the ride was not in total darkness as the fiberglass was somewhat translucent. The slides shared a waist-deep pool at the end of their courses and riders had to be at least 42 inches tall to participate. As an added perk for guests, there was no fee tacked on for the use of tubes for the lazy river or slides, something many other parks charged for.

When they first opened, the attractions allowed for single tubes and two-person rafts. However, the park soon realized that the two-person rafts on AmaZOOM were descending too fast and the operation was changed to single riders only.

Both slides were designed by New Jersey architect Fred Langford, who is considered by many in the amusement park industry to be the father of the modern-day water slides. Langford holds numerous patents and was the first to use fiberglass in his slide construction back in the 1980s, replacing the then standard use of concrete. In addition, he also invented a self-supporting beam system which allowed slides to be longer and more exciting than their predecessors.

H₂O Spelled Success

Splashin' Safari, though relatively small in comparison to other water parks in the nation at the time, was deemed a success in its first year of operation.

"It was well received by guests," Lori Koch recalled, though all three attractions are no longer part of the Splashin' Safari footprint. The two large water slides did find a new home at the adjoining Lake Rudolph Campground & RV Resort, which at the time was owned and operated by Will Koch's late brother, Philip. Congo River and Crocodile Isle were both demolished in 2012 to make way for a new entry plaza to the water park.

The second phase of Splashin' Safari made its debut for the 1994 season. The Wave pool was another attraction designed to gobble up as many guests as

Amusement Parks and Water

A Natural Combination

From the earliest days, amusement parks have always served as an escape from the summer heat. Water was often part of the equation as most early amusement parks featured a body of water—be it a small pond, a river, a lake, or the seashore—for visitors to take advantage of the cooling breezes. As the industry began to grow, rides utilizing water began to appear.

In 1817, Jardin Ruggieri in Paris introduced a Shoot-the-Chutes ride in which a boat slid down an incline into a pool of water. The concept was introduced in the United States in 1884 at Watch Tower Park in Rock Island, Illinois, where a wooden ramp was erected down a bluff from the park to the Rock River; flat-bottomed boats filled with riders slid down the ramp and into the water. The concept soon spread rapidly throughout the country and by the 1920s had evolved into the Mill Chute, which resembled today's Log Flume rides.

In 1923, Herbert Sellner, better known as the inventor of the Tilt-A-Whirl, created the Water-Toboggan Slide. It featured a wooden sled that individuals sat on and rode down an incline into a lake, making it one of the first widely produced water slides.

By now the industry was in a golden age in which increasingly thrilling rides began to dominate. Not only rides but swimming pools became a popular attraction at amusement parks. These were no mere backyard pools but huge swimming holes measuring hundreds of feet square that featured slides and even bleachers for spectators. Sunlite Pool at Coney Island in Cincinnati, Ohio, for instance, opened in 1925, measuring 200

feet by 400 feet, and remains as one of the last examples of an amusement park swimming pool from this era.

These huge pools fell out of favor as theme parks began to dominate the industry in the 1960s, but even theme park customers appreciated a good splashing. The need for a water ride that would fit the theme park environment was solved in 1963 when El Aserradero opened at Six Flags Over Texas. It was the first Log Flume, in which boats traveled down a water-filled fiberglass trough ending with a drop down a hill into a pool for a cooling splash. They quickly became a must-have attraction among theme parks and always ranked among their most popular attractions.

By now, water-based entertainment attractions were beginning to spread throughout the country. In 1969, Big Surf opened in Tempe, Arizona, featuring the first wave pool, while free standing water slide attractions started opening along roadsides throughout America. These primitive attractions featured gunite (a form of concrete) slides erected on a mound of dirt, which made widespread development impractical. In the late 1970s, however, Fred Langford, perfected the concept of a fiberglass water slide, forever changing the industry, and they began appearing as singular attractions in a handful of amusement parks.

The 1976 opening of River Country at Walt Disney World hinted at the potential of a water-based amusement park, but it took George Millay to create the water park as it exists today. In 1974, Millay left Sea World, the marine life theme park he had founded and started looking for his next great

The addition of the Wave significantly increased the acreage of Splashin' Safari. *Holiday World photo.*

opportunity. Seeing the growth of freestanding waterslides and wave pools, he developed the concept of a "water playground" where customers could spend the day cooling off in a variety of water-based attractions.

In 1977, Millay opened Wet 'n Wild in Orlando, considered the world's first water park, although that term was not used until 1979. A new industry literally was born overnight, and water parks rapidly spread throughout the world. But for the first several years, amusement parks and water parks were two separate and distinct concepts. People went to amusement parks to enjoy attractions in their clothes, while water parks required a swimming suit.

But that changed in 1983, when Geauga Lake in Aurora, Ohio, opened Boardwalk Shores, a full-scale water park. Rather than charging separate admission, it was fully integrated into the traditional amusement park. It was the first time the two separate concepts were combined into a single attraction for a single admission. While some were skeptical that the two concepts would complement each other, the public disagreed, and Geauga Lake had a huge 1983 season.

Operators around the world saw how successful combining amusement and water park attractions could be, and soon, rather than a novelty, combined amusement and water parks became the industry standard. It was an idea Holiday World embraced to the extreme with its ongoing development of Splashin' Safari.

possible at one time to meet the park's growing demand for water attractions.

The Wave, still operating at the park today, covers 21,000 square feet with water depth ranging from a mere splash at its shoreline to 6 feet when waves are released by a computerized operating system. Eight different wave patterns are generated in cycles lasting seven minutes before the system shuts down for ten minutes, allowing guests to catch their breath before the next series of waves is released. For a time, the park also operated a gentle wave pool, Butterfly Bay, adjacent to The Wave.

Bring on the Slides

While 1995 did not see an addition to the Splashin' Safari lineup, the park unveiled its first large wooden roller coaster, The Raven. The ride sparked additional interest in Holiday World not only among the general public but also groups of coaster enthusiasts who will travel great distances to catch the latest in thrill experiences.

The bump in attendance brought about by The Raven—the park set a record with nearly half-

Watubee was Splashin' Safari's first water slide in which families could ride together. *Holiday World photo.*

included a new major water slide for Splashin' Safari as well as an additional entrance and exit to the Congo River lazy river.

Will Koch reached out to ProSlide Technology, which had quickly become an industry leader after launching its first products in 1986. On the drawing boards was an enormous raft ride capable of holding up to five persons—a maximum of four adults—on one raft.

In October 1995, the park officially broke ground for the huge slide, with Will Koch at the helm of a bulldozer to move the first swath of earth at the project site.

He touted in a press release that the attraction, which the park named Watubee, would be the only such ride in Illinois, Kentucky, and Indiana. And since children just 36 inches tall could participate, Will emphasized that entire families could "Do the Watubee together." The media information also stated that an additional fifty seasonal jobs would be created to staff the slide during the park's season.

When completed, the $750,000 project stood six stories high with a trough width of 10 feet to accommodate the large rafts, which were more than 6 feet in diameter. The green fiberglass ride had a run of 625 feet and emptied into a splash pool with a depth of 30 inches. The large rafts made their way to the top of the launch platform via a conveyor system.

While the ride's name Watubee hints of an African or safari theme, Holiday World's website quips, Translation: None—we made it up!

When the 1996 season rolled around, Splashin' Safari had expanded to cover fifteen acres within the theme park's property and Holiday World anticipated a 10 percent increase in attendance due to the new high-profile water attraction.

"Watubee really took us to the next level—it really put us on the map," Leah Koch, a fourth-generation owner, said of the project. "During that time, we were expanding so rapidly."

a-million guests passing through the gates that season—likely helped to set the stage for further capital investments at Holiday World, including its water park.

According to park records, the property embarked on a $1.4 million expansion project for 1996, which

Riders traveled through Otorongo's three slides in complete darkness. *Holiday World photo.*

Leah, one of Lori and Will's three children, also serves as director of communications for Holiday World, while sister Lauren is director of entertainment and events, and brother William is director of technical production.

ProSlide apparently made a positive and lasting impression on the Koch family with the design and manufacture of Watubee, as the Canadian firm has been selected to produce every water slide at Holiday World since the '96 season. A number of those future projects propelled Splashin' Safari into obtaining world-class status among water attractions.

The 1996 season surpassed the projected 10 percent growth the Kochs had envisioned (attendance was up 15 percent) and on March 1, 1997, Will Koch announced that the park would invest another $2 million as it entered its fifty-second year.

In a press release issued by the business, he said higher capacity was at the heart of the decision and that three new water slides and two restaurants would be part of the capital expenditures. In addition, the family business was adding public camping at the adjacent Lake Rudolph Outdoor Resort, putting in what it called "class A" sites for overnight guests.

The new Splashin' Safari complex from ProSlide incorporated three ride-in-the-dark slides dropping from a 40-foot tower. Holiday World named the attraction Otorongo (otto-RON-go) after a rare Peruvian Jaguar, and wittily, the slides were called Otto, Ron, and Go with lengths of 179, 260 and 326 feet. Riders mount double-tubes before taking the plunge into darkness, with each slide offering a different experience. All three slides share a splash pool with a depth of nearly 4 feet.

Monsoon Season

"Adding capacity" was a term often used when Will Koch talked about new attractions coming to the family's Indiana business. As the crowds grew over the years, Holiday World remained focused on keeping up with the public's ever-growing appetite for more rides and water elements.

And increasing capacity had been a key to the success for the park so guests could get their fill of fun without waiting hours in a staggering line to participate on a single attraction.

As a testament to that philosophy, Holiday World & Splashin' Safari had grown from a day-visit property to a destination park before the new millennium arrived.

"People started coming in wanting to do the dry park one day and the water park another," Leah Koch noted. "As we increased the water park attractions, we increased attendance."

In December of 1997, Will Koch made an announcement that the park would again invest in Splashin' Safari to increase capacity but this time by constructing the largest interactive water play and slide complex in the state.

Called Monsoon Lagoon, the new addition for the '98 season was really the jungle gym of water attractions as it provided a dozen multitiered platforms with a variety of interactions for patrons.

Monsoon Lagoon was a large play area highlighted by regular dumps of a 1,000-gallon bucket. *Holiday World photo.*

Monsoon Lagoon, designed by the former SCS Interactive of Englewood, Colorado, was heavily themed and really fit nicely into the safari motif the park was leaning toward. While engineers at SCS Interactive were experts in designing all of the unique spray and fountain elements in the structure, ProSlide was contracted to build the attraction's four body slides. The structure had a footprint about the size of a basketball court with a large area in the front decked out with loungers so adults could relax while the youngsters were busy trying out the sixty different ways to get soaked.

Monsoon Lagoon was a staple at Holiday World for 21 seasons before being replaced by a similar project.

The 1998 season was special in another way as industry publication *Amusement Today* (AT) honored Holiday World with a Golden Ticket Award for being named the Friendliest Park on the planet. AT's annual Golden Ticket Awards pay tribute to what is said to be the "Best Of The Best" in the amusement industry with results compiled by a panel of experienced theme park enthusiasts from around the world. The Arlington, Texas, publication has presented its Golden Ticket Awards since 1998 and since then, Holiday World has racked up more than its share of accolades.

Water on the Back Burner, But Not for Long

By the close of the '98 season, Splashin' Safari had branched out to cover eighteen acres within the park property and could entertain up to 7,500 guests an hour. And for the visionary Will Koch Jr., there must have been a genuine sense of accomplishment seeing that new side of the business sprout to such huge success in less than a decade.

As for rural Santa Claus, Indiana, the explosive growth at Holiday World fueled other business opportunities—especially in accommodations—in

It included water cannons, cascading fountains, water wheels, and four tame body slides. At center stage was a huge tipping bucket looming over guests standing on the concrete pad below. Every few minutes the pail would empty a deluge of one thousand gallons of water on the anxiously waiting crowd.

The addition of Zoombabwe (aka the purple people eater) increased the size of Splashin' Safari by four acres. *Holiday World photo.*

the community of around two thousand residents at that time.

"They were badly needed," Leah Koch said of the local hotels constructed for vacationing families. "We also saw some new restaurants during that era, but unfortunately they come and go—it's hard for them to survive when we are just open for the summer."

Improvements for 1999 shifted away from the water park as a new themed area titled Holidog's FunTown was added to the 4th of July section of Holiday World. Holiday World was again named

Friendliest Park when the '99 Golden Ticket Awards were presented.

Numerous guest services improvements were made in 2001 as the park reached another milestone with more than 600,000 persons passing through the gates. Seasonal employment also topped 1,000 for the first time in 2001.

Splashin' Safari was back in the news for 2002 as the park announced it would build the world's largest enclosed water slide. The $1.7 million ride was also the largest single project in the water park's history.

Called ZOOMbabwe—another name the park made up for yucks to fit the safari theme—the behemoth slide was nearly 900 feet in length when completed. Plunging more than 100 feet from the launch tower, the twisting and turning course incorporates six steep drops in its fiberglass tube, which is up to an impressive 12 feet in diameter. The ride lasts an exhilarating 50 seconds from start to finish, splashing down in three feet of water.

This "purple people eater" of water attractions can swallow up to one thousand guests per hour, thanks to the use of twenty-four cloverleaf-shaped rafts capable of holding up to four persons. It also increased the size of Splashin' Safari by four acres, bringing to twenty-two the total number of acres covered by the water park.

ZOOMbabwe was designed from ProSlide's existing MAMMOTH platform. When ProSlide introduced MAMMOTH in 1996, it was honored by the International Association of Amusement Parks and Attractions (IAAPA) with a Brass Ring Award for Best New Water Park Ride.

Holiday World added another park perk for the 2002 season with free sunscreen for all guests. That was a big plus, especially for families basking under the sun while enjoying Splashin' Safari for the day.

Not Bazinga, It's Just Plain Zinga

The park closed 2002 with an astonishing 20 percent increase in attendance, and Will Koch again said the park needed to increase capacity.

"As we grow, we're determined to keep lines short and families happy," he said in a press release announcing new attractions for both Splashin' Safari and Holiday World for 2003. The $3.8 million earmarked for the additions would be the largest amount in the park's fifty-eight-year history and would include another major water slide in Splashin'

Zinga was one of the first water slides to utilize a giant funnel. *Holiday World photo.*

Jungle Racer allows ten guests at a time to race each other. *Holiday World photo.*

Safari, which now covered twenty-four acres and could entertain up to 9,300 guests per hour.

With ProSlide again charged with building the new water ride, Holiday World selected the manufacturer's TORNADO 60, an attraction like nothing seen before at the property—or for that matter at any water park on the planet.

Appropriately named Zinga by Holiday World, the title is a Swahili word meaning to move in a circle.

ProSlide holds a patent on the reducing-radius funnel used on its Tornado rides, with 60 feet in diameter being the largest it produces. The Holiday World project was one of the first using ProSlide's giant funnel, also referred to as a half-pipe on the park's website.

Zinga, standing 78 feet tall, thrusts its rafts into the funnel from the tunneled helix slide, and they swoop back and forth across the gigantic cone, creating moments of zero gravity between the intense drops. After oscillating in the funnel several times, the four-person rafts then plunge into fog effects in the final section of tunnel before coming to rest in the splash pool. The 40-second ride has a capacity of up to 720 guests an hour.

Those weary of taking the plunge have the opportunity to observe riders get washed in the enormous funnel from an observation deck.

Amusement Today named Zinga the Best Water Park Ride at its 2003 Golden Ticket Awards. ProSlide also won the 2003 IAAPA Impact Award for the TORNADO 60 (new ride) installation at Holiday World & Splashin' Safari. According to Phil Hayles, vice president for business development and strategic accounts for ProSlide, the company installed two other TORNADO 60s concurrently as the Holiday World project was completed, but Splashin' Safari's was the largest, with a run of 336 feet.

It's A Jungle Out There

Coming off a string of banner seasons, Holiday World & Splashin' Safari wasted no time in pumping more capital investment into its venerable water park for 2004.

The park announced that $3.2 million in improvements would be made throughout the property, with most of the expenditure going into two new attractions for Splashin' Safari.

"We again looked for high-capacity water rides and activities," Will Koch said in an April 2004 press release. "We want families to know they can spend a day here having fun—not standing in line."

To make good on that promise, the park built Jungle Racer, which is a colorful array of ten water slide lanes perfectly aligned to make it a racetrack of wet rides. Standing five stories high with each slide 314 feet in length, riders race on toboggan-style foam mats to the finish line where an electronic scoreboard announces the winners. Jungle Racer is from ProSlide's ProRACER lineup and was the first-ever ten-lane installment and remains the only one in the world today. The ProRACER won the 1994 IAAPA honors as best new water park ride.

The park's website teasingly states, "It seems that Dads always win!" The comment was probably posted to generate its fair share of family competition on the attraction.

To satisfy parents with younger children, a "sprayground" named Jungle Jets was built adjacent to Jungle Racer and incorporated more than one hundred sixty water jets, spray arches, and other get-wet features. It was constructed by Waterworks International of Kankakee, Illinois.

The jungle area at Splashin' Safari also had a new restaurant, restrooms, and deck area to better serve guests that season. The new additions made their debut on May 15 and—in another move to meet a growing demand among parents—Holiday World became a nonsmoking facility.

The park also installed a conveyor system to move the large clover leaf tubes to the top of the Zinga water slide tower. Before that, the task fell on the shoulders of the guests as they had to tote them up the stairway. Phew!

A Deluge of Additions

By the close of the 2004 season, a record 883,000 guests had passed through the gates, and the Koch family was in "nothing's going to stop us now" mode as a flurry of additions came to the table for both the dry and water park.

"It was a tidal wave of growth," Leah Koch said of the seasons that followed. "For sure, much of the growth we were witnessing parkwide was due to the success of the water park."

"When we announced the opening of Splashin' Safari for the 1993 season, we never dreamed how successful it would be," Will Koch was quoted in a May 2005 press release. "We have added to it nearly every year since and for the 2005 season are launching an expansion that will eventually make it twice as big."

Included in the $6.3 million in 2005 projects was an additional wave pool for Splashin' Safari. Named Bahari, meaning immense sea in Swahili, the colossal pool covered nearly three-quarters of an acre when completed and was almost twice the size of the Wave, the 1994 installment. The family attraction incorporated geysers, sprays, and jets and—of course—computer-generated wave patterns up to four feet high. The $2.1 million Bahari complex, which included a beach area, food service, and peninsula with gushing geysers, added six acres to Splashin' Safari and was constructed by Aquatic Development Group of Cohoes, New York.

Holiday World marked its sixtieth anniversary in 2006 and wasted no time in bolstering its offerings in both parks. The expansion—to the tune of $13.5 million—would be the largest in the park's history with a jaw-dropping roller coaster (The Voyage) to be constructed in the new Thanksgiving section of the theme park and an action river added to Splashin' Safari.

The new Bahari River provided a little more excitement than the park's existing Congo River lazy river as it had stronger currents and a number of waterfalls. Marketed as a family attraction for all ages, the inner tube ride was 1,100 feet in length with a depth of 28 inches when completed.

The investments paid dividends as they pushed Holiday World & Splashin' Safari attendance over the one-million mark for the first time.

By the mid-2000s, Splashin' Safari was emerging as one of the largest water parks in the country. *Holiday World photo*.

Time to Bowl and Monkey Business

Adding more big thrills to the Splashin' Safari arsenal was next on the park's agenda for the 2007 season.

ProSlide was again contracted to build the new attraction from its BehemothBOWL 60 platform—hyped to be "the world's largest family bowl experience." It was slated to be part of Holiday World's $4.5 million in improvements for the upcoming season.

"Again, the 60 represents feet, which is the widest portion of the bowl, which is 60 feet in diameter," ProSlide's Phil Hayles said of the project. Holiday World named the ride Bakuli, which is Swahili for bowl.

Riders on four-person cloverleaf tubes plunge from atop a 73-foot tower through more than 300 feet of enclosed (dark) fiberglass slide before being hurled into the gigantic bowl. The rafts whip around the bowl multiple times before riders drop through the center of the basin and into the splash pool for exiting. ProSlide holds a patent on the corkscrew bowl-exit design.

"This was our second IAAPA Impact Award winner at ProSlide," Hayles noted. "And low and behold, the Holiday World installation took that in."

The park's attendance for the season again topped one million guests.

More interactive water play was the key element on the radar for Splashin' Safari when plans for the 2008 season were announced. Holiday World was continuing its aggressive reinvestment campaign with $6 million earmarked throughout the property, of which $1.7 million would be spent in Splashin' Safari.

Drawing off the success of its Monsoon Lagoon modular play structure, the park was set to install a similar themed area, which would appeal to younger families. Named Kima Bay, the attraction would have—count' em—more than one hundred water-play elements incorporated into its four-story structure including more than 125 water jets, seven small water slides, and a 1,200-gallon tipping bucket.

In announcing the project, Will Koch said, "We think children will especially enjoy the fun monkey theming, nearly as much as the climbing, splashing and sliding in store for them at Kima Bay."

He went on to say that the modular unit will help increase capacity in the water park, one of his ongoing priorities.

It was built by Whitewater West Industries of Richmond, British Columbia, Canada. In 2005 Whitewater acquired SCS Interactive, which built Splashin' Safari's Monsoon Lagoon.

A Water Coaster? New Era For Holiday World & Splashin' Safari

There's no doubt that the laws of physics play a vital roll in the design of roller coasters, and those thrill rides are one of the biggest draws for amusement and theme parks.

Taking Splashin' Safari to the next level was something Will Koch had apparently been pondering for some time before the 2010 season, and to accomplish that, the park needed the latest and greatest innovation in H_2O attractions.

During that time, water coaster—yes, you read it correctly, water coaster—technology had been emerging in the industry with ProSlide again at the forefront.

"Dad actually waited until the technology was up to his standards," Leah Koch recalled as Holiday World was preparing to announce it would build the world's longest water coaster for the 2010 season.

Appropriately named Wildebeest, the ride was to be more than 1,700 feet long and to have seven

By the late-2000s, Splashin' Safari had grown to the point it needed a second play area, and Kima Bay was added. The Tembo complex (*top*), a kiddie area followed in 2018. *Holiday World photo.*

drops totaling 178 feet, two underground tunnels, and a helix. What made the ride a "water coaster" was the fact that the four-person rafts would actually be pushed up seven hills through the use of linear induction motors (LIMs). The theme park industry was introduced to this state-of-the-art launch system in 1996 when two roller coasters made their debut using LIMs.

But applying the technology to water slides was another thing, until ProSlide engineers got their mitts on it. The company designed and perfected the use of LIMs for a new line it marketed as the HydroMAGNETIC ROCKET.

"I worked extensively with Will and ProSlide in building Wildebeest," said Lori Gogel, who was director of Splashin' Safari from 1997 to 2014.

The sprawling Wildebeest brought Splashin' Safari to a whole new level. *Holiday World photo.*

"ProSlide came up with the design, but I sat in on the meetings and pointed out other things we needed on the attractions, such as cameras."

Today, she is the director of revenue administration, a long way from her start at Holiday World in 1994 as a lifeguard.

As ProSlide's Phil Hayles further explained the state-of-the-art workings behind Wildebeest, he pointed out that the LIMs in the company's product are encased within the uphill fiberglass LIM sections.

"In the base of the boats are steel plates, and when they pass over the LIMs it creates a series of magnetic pulls and pushes—many, many times in a second," he noted. "We space the motors so it's absolutely seamless from a speed perspective and that speed remains constant."

Hayles said the company basically adopted the technology behind LIMs in roller coasters to make the HydroMAGNETIC ROCKET a reality. Once the boats are lifted to the top of the conveyor, gravity and the LIMs take over for the remainder of the ride and—voilà!—you have a water coaster.

"We were the first to use LIM technology in a water ride," he continued. "Will Koch, who was an early adopter of ProSlide's new product innovations, waited to ensure that LIM technology worked seamlessly."

Leah Koch agreed with that assessment, stating, "Dad's wait-and-see decision worked out for the best."

Wildebeest, a $5.5 million project, opened May 14, 2010, to much fanfare and worldwide industry attention. ProSlide's chairman and chief executive officer Rick Hunter, who was always instrumental and had his hands in all aspects of Splashin' Safari designs, also made his way to Holiday World to look over the huge attraction shortly after it made its debut.

Sadly, Will Koch, 48, passed away unexpectedly only weeks later.

By the close of the 2010 season, park attendance again surpassed the one-million mark, and that fall, Wildebeest was named the World's #1 Water Park Ride and Best New Water Park ride at the AT's Golden Ticket Awards. The addition of the new water attraction also boosted Splashin' Safari's footprint to 27 acres.

More for the Younger Generation and Then a Mammoth

Other members of the Koch family took the helm in directing Holiday World & Splashin' Safari into 2011, apparently taking a chapter from Will Koch's formula for success.

ProSlide was again contracted to provide eight slides for children that would be incorporated into a new Splashin' Safari area called Safari Sam's Splashland. The attraction would have a mix of open

Top, Next to Mammoth is Bahari, Splashin' Safari's second wave pool, added in 2005. *Holiday World photo.*

Above, At 1,763 feet, Mammoth was certified by the *Guinness Book of World Records* as the world's longest water coaster. *Holiday World photo.*

Splashin' Safari's second water coaster, Mammoth, truly lived up to its name. *Holiday World photo.*

and enclosed slides, all of which emptied into a large wading pool with spray arches and other wet features.

As Will Koch had instilled in the business model years before his death, it was critical to increase capacity while ensuring that the guest experience is the best it can be. The new Splashland for youngsters fulfilled that agenda for 2011.

Later that summer Holiday World, coming off the previous year's monumental success of Wildebeest, announced that it would construct another water coaster in Splashin' Safari for 2012.

"We had had several huge capital investments before then," Leah Koch recalled. "But Mammoth was the largest at $12 million."

The colossal, three-minute ride would run 1,763 feet—a third of a mile—edging out Wildebeest by just 53 feet (1,710) to reign as the world's longest water coaster. After a conveyor lifted the six-passenger rafts to a height of 69 feet, the course would include seven drops with the boats propelled to the top of the ensuing hills by linear induction motors. Six LIMs, including the longest ever put on a water coaster, were incorporated into the design as well as five tunnels.

Mammoth, covering three acres in Splashin' Safari, officially opened on May 11, 2012. In 2017, the ride was certified in the *Guinness Book of World Records* as the World's Longest Water Coaster.

Holiday World also introduced cabana rentals, themed Bahari River Cabanas, for the first time in 2012 as an added amenity in Splashin' Safari. Eric Snow, vice president and chief marketing officer for Holiday World, managed the cabana project, including concept development and research.

"Will wasn't sure about putting in something exclusive like that as he wanted everyone to have the

The Makings of the Mammoth

Building a Mammoth had to be a monumental task, and we went right to the experts at ProSlide Technology for the lowdown on what it took to put this world-record water coaster together.

So here are the nuts and bolts (pun intended) of the humongous project at Holiday World & Splashin' Safari:

· 62 truckloads of fiberglass trough sections

· Four additional trucks delivered the conveyor and controls

· There are a total of 92 LIM boosters (linear induction motors) incorporated along the ride in six different locations. The largest has 22 boosters, the longest on any water coaster in the world

· 76 spread footings were put into place to help support the structure

· 104 concrete pedestals had to be poured to cement the deal, 90 of which support the actual ride and 13 the conveyor system

· The ride covers more than three acres

· And—finally—we didn't forget the hardware: It took 45,805 sets of nuts and bolts to put Mammoth together

Did the instruction manual say "some assembly required?"

Wildebeest (*left*) and Mammoth (*right*) put Splashin' Safari on the map as the water coaster capital. *Holiday World photo.*

same experience," Lori Koch said of the shelters. "It worked out as people love them."

As the popularity of the rentals increased, the park added additional units with thirty-nine available to date throughout the expansive water park. And, "Yes, they sell out on most days," Leah Koch noted.

A Laughing Matter for a While

Holiday World & Splashin' Safari did introduce another water slide complex for the 2013 season. Called Hyena Falls, it consisted of three ProSlide PIPElines and a ProSlide PIPElineWAVE. All four raft/tube slides had enclosed areas along their runs, and Hyena Falls was touted as an in-the-dark attraction.

The PIPElineWAVE was the most unique slide in Hyena Falls as it utilized ProSlide's gigantic curved wall. After riders dropped into that feature of the ride, they were swept across the top of the wall and experienced zero g's.

The same year, *USA Today* named Splashin' Safari the best water park in the world.

Hyena Falls had a short history at Holiday World, in part because it was situated in a rather obscure location in relation to the rest of Splashin' Safari. The attraction was officially retired at the close of the 2019 season.

Also in 2013, long-time employee Matt Eckert was named president and chief executive officer by the park's board of directors. He had served as the property's controller and a general manger prior to the promotion.

There were no plans for additional attractions in Splashin' Safari for 2014, but the water park did add Wildebeestro, where gourmet burgers, fresh fruit, and salads were served up. In addition, the Safari Outpost retail shop was also built.

Later that year, Wildebeest was again named the World's #1 Water Park Ride by *Amusement Today*.

Taking Care of Business

While Splashin' Safari has a relatively short season each year, taking care of business is a year-round task for the maintenance staff at the water park.

"We have divided our rides maintenance team into the North Shop and the South Shop," noted Holiday World's Leah Koch, director of communications and a fourth-generation owner.

The North Shop is assigned to Splashin' Safari as well as the Thunderbird roller coaster in the dry park. It takes seven full-time employees just to maintain all of the workings in the dozens of water slides, countless spray cannons, and other water elements in Splashin' Safari when the park is operational. Off-season, there's plenty to do as attraction components have to be winterized, cleaned, and prepped for the coming year.

There are nearly forty full-time employees in the maintenance department, which include painters, carpenters, and technicians.

No doubt, it takes a lot of behind-the-scenes teamwork to keep a theme park running.

Facing, Cheetah Chase rounded out Splashin' Safari's trio of water coasters. *Holiday World photo.*

More for the Little Squirts

In a November 2017 press release, Holiday World & Splashin' Safari announced that Christmas would be arriving a little early as Santa's bag of goodies included two new water park elements for the upcoming season.

"We're adding a fun elephant-themed water-play area for younger children," said Eckert. "When we discovered the Swahili word for elephant is Tembo, we named our new slide complex Tembo Falls and the junior wave pool Tembo Tides."

The two water attractions were part of Holiday World's $3.5 million in 2018 spending allocated throughout the park.

Tembo Falls was to be geared toward kids under 54 inches and included eight ProSlide junior body slides, five of which were enclosed KIDZ Twisters, plus a MiniRiver, a KIDZ ProRACER, and a KIDZ BOWL.

"Holiday World is one of the few parks that has two very large kids' zones," ProSlide's Phil Hayles commented. "Safari Sam's Splashland was super, super successful for them, so Tembo Falls was a natural addition."

The embellishments led to more accolades for the park in 2019, with *USA Today* again naming Splashin' Safari the best water park in the nation and online travel and review website TripAdvisor inducting Holiday World & Splashin' Safari into its hall of fame.

The Chase Is On! And the Winner Is?

In early August of 2019, Holiday World & Splashin' Safari held a press conference that was an eye-opener throughout the theme park industry.

Splashin' Safari was preparing to add its third water coaster and in sticking to the safari theme, it would be named Cheetah Chase. The ride would actually be two racing slides totaling more than 1,700 feet using ProSlide's RocketBLAST technology.

ProSlide's dueling RocketBLAST won the IAAPA Impact Award.

"Cheetah Chase is the perfect thrill ride for families. The three-person rafts allow families to race face-to-face, and the launch is the first of its kind," the park's Matt Eckert said in announcing the addition. "There's nothing like this out there."

Indeed, there was nothing like it in business as Cheetah Chase would have a water-powered flat launch that would send its toboggan-style rafts racing toward a black-and-white (alternating sections of fiberglass) finish line, making it the first full-circuit racing water coaster.

Another "first-ever" would be a head-to-head dueling race zone and two RallyPOINTS—another ProSlide innovation—where the rafts would synchronize with one another. Each slide would also have two FlyingSAUCER elements, which produce a faster ride with a drop-and-dive sensation with guests glued to the wall by centrifugal forces.

"When Holiday World reached out to us (ProSlide), they were looking at an underdeveloped area of the park for a new attraction," asserted Hayles. "I did a walk through with James Olliver, who was vice president of park operations at the time. He told me, 'We're looking to revamp an underutilized area of the park—we want to do something really cool here.'"

The $7 million installment would include the tallest RocketBLAST section in the world at 27 feet. In all, five sections of the ride included the RocketBLAST technology, in which the rafts are propelled using targeted water nozzles rather than the linear induction motors used on Wildebeest and Mammoth.

"The biggest boosts we saw in attendance were the years we introduced Wildebeest and Mammoth," Leah Koch added. "So, we said, 'Let's do that again,' and that led to Cheetah Chase."

"With the addition of Cheetah Chase, Splashin' Safari will now be the undisputed water coaster capital of the world," Eckert noted during the press conference.

The ride opened to an abbreviated 2020 season due to the COVID pandemic sweeping the globe.

While Leah Koch offered assurance that more attractions are likely to be added in coming years at the Indiana property, one thing is for certain: a key ingredient to Holiday World and Splashin' Safari's recipe for success was to **Just add water**!

Facing, Cheetah Chase is a unique twin-trough water coaster that allows friends and families to race each other.
Zach Dobson photo.

Looking Forward

A New Generation Comes to Holiday World

Leah Koch

In summer 2010, Holiday World & Splashin' Safari felt unstoppable. My dad, Will Koch, had just built Wildebeest, the World's Longest Water Coaster. Kentucky Kingdom in Louisville, Kentucky, had announced that it would not reopen for the 2010 season, and we had one chance with first-time visitors to win them over before they traveled a little farther to Cincinnati.

Holiday World was partnering with the nearby Lincoln Amphitheatre to create a new show: *A. Lincoln*. The goal was to help people decide to stay for two days rather than one: guests could enjoy the park for the day, then drive over to the amphitheater for more free unlimited soft drinks and Holiday World concessions at the show and stay nearby to enjoy the park for a second day following. It was all a part of the grand plan to make Santa Claus, Indiana, a true destination.

You could feel the electricity of the momentum my dad had built. Guests and employees alike believed in the park and in my dad's vision. We may not have all known what the next thing would be, but we all knew it was important and that we were in the midst of something very special.

My siblings and I were all working at the park. Lauren was returning from her junior year at Florida State to perform in our stage shows, William had just finished his sophomore year of high school and was running sound for our shows, and I was home from my freshman year at Indiana University, sharing my time between shows and interning for Communications. I was working for the legendary Paula Werne—who had been telling and shaping the story of Holiday World beautifully for two decades at that time. I had a front-row seat to see my dad in interviews sharing about his newest addition, Wildebeest.

I remember Paula forwarded an email to me one day with the subject line, "Your Daughter." I panicked when I saw she had sent it to my dad and forwarded his response to me. Had I walked past a piece of trash in the midway without noticing and picking it up? Were my shoes not perfectly white? I opened it to find a message that Paula had written, "Your Daughter is quite the photographer. Can I keep her?" One of the photos I had taken in my capacity as intern was attached. And my dad had replied that he would need me back at some point. It was small, but it felt like I was carving out a place for myself in the company. That I might be able to return someday. And that I might like it.

My dad had been planning for that, too. He had slowly purchased his siblings' shares in the company and was drafting documents so if something were to

Chronology

2010
President Will Koch passed away unexpectedly in June.

2011
Rudolph's Round Up in the Christmas section replaced Blitzen's Airplanes. Free Wi-Fi hotspots are placed throughout both parks

2012
The Sparkler vertical swing ride is added to the 4th of July section, replacing Paul Revere's Midnight Ride. Rock the World Christian Music fest premiers and the park's calendar expands to include Happy Halloween Weekends. Freedom Train is retired after 65 years of service

2013
Kitty's Tea Party is added to Holidog's FunTown. The Holidog Express train replaced the Freedom Train. Longtime employee Matt Eckert is named President and CEO

2014
Mayflower swinging ship ride opened in Thanksgiving. Mrs. Klaus's Kitchen gets a theming redo. On July 24, after *66 Days at Sea*, more than a thousand gather to watch the announcement of Thunderbird, the nation's first launched wing coaster

2015
Thunderbird, the nation's first launched wing coaster, premieres April 25. Sparkler moved to Thanksgiving and renamed Crow's Next

2016
Park celebrates its 70th Birthday Season with the addition of the 70th Birthday Plaza, displaying the park's retired Freedom Train, along with the Memories Mosaic, made from 7,000 photos from over the park's seven decades

2017
Firecracker, a classic Calypso ride, is rescued and restored

2019
Santa's Merry Marketplace replaced Kringle's Kafé, expanding the restaurant size by 50 percent with menus to include old favorites and new cuisine

2020
Holiday World hosts a "digital opening day" due to COVID-19 operating restrictions. The official park opening was delayed until June 14

Mayflower was added to Holiday World's Thanksgiving section in 2014. *Holiday World photo.*

happen to him, we could remain involved or we could sell his shares and use the money to pursue different dreams. He was planning to talk to my siblings and me that summer to figure out if we were interested in remaining involved.

But his time was cut short. My father, Will Koch Jr., passed away on June 13. The shock waves rocked our family, town, and state. The park had suddenly lost its visionary. While the season carried on, and we broke attendance records, the whole place felt . . . lost.

My family and I quickly had to choose whether we wanted to sell his shares or to dive into the park. We wanted to carry on Dad's vision, and we still do.

It was a complicated time, but I remember realizing—in between taking finals my senior year of college—that our time to lead had come. And we needed help.

We appointed Matt Eckert, who had been one of two general managers for Dad, as park president—the first ever "Koch Family Outsider" to take on the role.

Mom, Lauren, William, and I formed our board of directors, and we asked Chip Cleary of Splish Splash in Long Island, and former IAAPA president and CEO, to join as well. Chip taught us to be good stewards of our assets, to be good operators, and to be true to what Holiday World was and is. Without Chip, the rest of this chapter would be a very different story.

No new attractions were scheduled for 2014 at the time, but by summer of 2013, we knew we needed to show that our family would continue to invest in the park. We were already in the planning stages for what would become Thunderbird, but we signed on with Chance Rides to build Mayflower, a swinging ship ride.

Why Steel?

Some kids beg their parents for a new phone, or a new car.

We begged our dad for a steel roller coaster.

I fell in love with inverted steel coasters, the type where the train travels beneath the track, at Universal's Islands of Adventure in Orlando when I was about 11. When I rode the Dueling Dragons coasters, I found myself suddenly unafraid of the coasters I never thought I'd ride. I had only kind-of adjusted to The Legend the year before—Fire and Ice, the names given to Dueling Dragon's twin tracks—will always hold a special place in my heart.

But I wasn't alone. Lauren and William also enjoyed a great inverted coaster as well. We had collectively harassed Dad for some sort of steel coaster for years. At some point after The Voyage was built, I started a more active campaign. I was finishing my freshman year when The Voyage opened. I asked my dad to build a steel coaster for me as a high school graduation present.

It didn't work, obviously. That said, he would occasionally bring drawings home and concept test with us. As a know-it-all teenager, I thought *anything* that went upside-down was cool and everything else was a waste of time (I'll admit I was incorrect. However, I still love a classic loop or a zero-g roll). Something about a steel coaster felt no less than perfect. It was something that came from our hearts. We knew Dad wanted to build a steel coaster—if nothing else, to shut us up—but the timing hadn't been right in his lifetime.

Instead of his gift to us, it was our gift to him.

The Big-Picture Decisions behind Thunderbird

I like to tell the story of developing Thunderbird through the lens of three battles I fought intensely and lost. And why I'm glad I lost every last one of them.

Early in summer 2013, we reached out to Bolliger & Mabillard (B & M) of Switzerland, which is considered one of the most innovative and highest-quality roller coaster designers on the planet. Dad had planned a few different steel coasters through the years, and we had seen several versions of coasters from several different vendors through the years. But he had landed on a B&M inverted coaster not long before he passed.

We asked Walter Bolliger to pull the most recent plans he and Dad had discussed, and we started from there.

We knew building a steel coaster would be popular with our regular guests and less popular with our roller coaster enthusiast guests. But we also knew we were not going to out-design the Voyage. So, we stuck to what we know Holiday World coasters do best: let the land tell us where to build and cut down as few trees as possible.

With that in mind, we also knew that Dad had a dream of one day creating a roller coaster that captured the energy of the Ewok flight in Star Wars:

Thunderbird represented the development of an entirely new area of Holiday World. *Holiday World photo.*

agile, fast, and close to the ground. The rest of our family hopped on board the wing coaster train. A wing coaster is a type of roller coaster where the seats ride not on top of the track but hang out over the sides.

I fought. To be clear, I did not necessarily fight because I disliked wing coasters—I hadn't ridden one at the time. I fought because of the concentration of such a unique breed of coaster that already existed in the Midwest. In Chicago at Six Flags Great America, there was X-Flight. In Sandusky, Ohio, at Cedar Point, there was Gatekeeper. In Pigeon Forge, Tennessee, at Dollywood, there was Wild Eagle. That's a lot of one type of coaster almost exclusively in our region. I fought for something different, or at the very least, something that would differentiate Thunderbird from the other coasters, because we couldn't afford to build the longest, tallest, or fastest. But my family was convinced the wing coaster—with nothing above or below riders—was exactly what Dad had been waiting for, *and* it was a family-friendly coaster model that still feels like a major roller coaster.

This loss was a half-loss. I lost the wing battle, but I won the differentiation battle. The launch was born out of conversations like this at our board and executive levels—for the record, in no way was the launch my idea. Once we knew we were moving forward with the launch, we changed the path of direction from the last B & M plans from Dad (the location would have been the same, but the lift hill would have traveled backward from the station today). The elements began to take shape. B & M ultimately helped us pick the layout we have—with the launch into the Immelmann element right over the path.

Facing top, Thunderbird was the first wing coaster to launch its trains out of the station (the flat section of track on the lower left). *Holiday World photo.*

Facing bottom, Like The Voyage, Holiday World prioritized maintaining as many trees as possible when building Thunderbird. *Holiday World photo.*

Above, Following the launch, Thunderbird travels straight into an Immelmann element, which is named after an aerobatic maneuver. *Holiday World photo.*

Eventually roller coaster connoisseurs would come to agree: what makes Thunderbird the best wing coaster (and yes, I can declare that—it's my chapter) is the fact that we had to shorten the trains to make the launch work. And the five-car train versus the seven-car train whips through the course with better pacing than the rest.

The next battle I lost? The name game. I've always been fascinated with the lost colony of Roanoke and I was convinced we could find something in that story that fit with the Thanksgiving section. The best I could come up with was the word "Croatoan" which

was inscribed on a tree after the colony went missing. While the mystery of that colony will eternally fascinate me, I realize I'm in the minority. After someone pointed out to me the multitude of ways our fans would mess up the name, I changed my mind. I'm glad I lost this one.

When it came to naming this attraction, nothing felt quite right. President and CEO Matt Eckert was the one who started to campaign for Thunderbird. We had paid a few companies to suggest names and none of them jumped out at us. Thunderbird was in one of those lists and because I am a lover of cryptozoology and mythology, the name started to speak to me. The fascination grew as I realized that the large bird that flapped its wings to make thunder was documented across time, peoples, and places. We learned that the 66-day journey the pilgrims took across the Atlantic was plagued by horrible storms toward the end, and I concocted a story of a Thunderbird that nearly wiped the pilgrims out but ultimately guided them to shore.

PGAV Destinations, out of St. Louis, Missouri, helped us design the station and surrounding buildings and helped us refine and craft the story of this time and place: our coaster station would be the farm of a descendant of one of the original Pilgrims who attempted to harness the power of the bird, sometimes with prosperous success, and sometimes with desolate repercussions.

The PGAV team told a better story, so I let it go and moved on.

My final stand may have been my greatest. We had decided on the type of coaster and the name and the theme of the section.

But what *color* would the coaster be?

My answer: a deep, dark, almost-green shade of blue. Like the color of a sky before a storm. To this day, I have no idea what color the supports would have been, and what color the trains would have been, so clearly it was a half-baked idea at best. But I knew in my gut it had to be *blue*.

PGAV suggested we pick between four shades of orange with brown supports. The brown supports, they said, would make the supports blend with the surrounding wooded areas, and make the track look like an orange ribbon floating in the woods. The train, then, would be a bluish color that would match the sky. After all, why has no one *caught* a Thunderbird if it doesn't blend in with the sky?

I would have none of it, but eventually, Lauren got me on board. And I found myself standing in the sun scrutinizing three tiny color samples to imagine what 3,000 feet of track would look like. If you think picking a paint color for a wall is difficult. Try picking one for a coaster. Lauren chose brilliantly.

Yet again I was wrong, but it couldn't have been such a stunning, beautiful, and family-perfect coaster had I won any of these strong stances I took.

For the record, I no longer make any color choices.

67 Days at Sea

We were sitting on the biggest secret ever kept in Holiday World history and had to figure out how best to announce it to the world. We had learned through developing the story behind the coaster that the original voyage over the Atlantic took the pilgrims 66 days, an idea arose: we would "journal" as one of the passengers and reveal some clues throughout the summer, leading up to our announcement day July 24, 2014—the day before bright orange steel was supposed to arrive at Holiday World.

To make sure no leaks got out, we kept the group of people in the know very tight, revealing the details only as we deemed it necessary (for example, the communications department had to help organize the release of information and build webpages for the announcement, so we revealed the information when the time came).

We happened to have a roller coaster enthusiast event on May 15, and we kicked off our *66 Days at Sea* campaign on May 19 by pretending to find a buried box in the woods that contained the "journal" from which we would base our campaign.

For *66 Days*, Director of Communications Paula Werne wrote a journal entry from our fictional passenger's perspective. The communications team and I developed a treatment for photos to make them look like drawings in the journal. The only thing the pilgrims saw for most of the 66 days was clouds, water, and boats. That's all there was to it.

Thunderbird Fact Sheet

Opened	April 25, 2015
Design company	Bolliger & Mabilliard Consulting Engineers, Monthey, Switzerland
Coaster type	Launched wing coaster
Launch technology	Linear synchronous motors
Length	3,035 feet
Maximum height	140 feet
Inversions	Four—Immelmann loop, vertical loop, horseshoe inversion, 360-degree inline twist
Headchopper "keyholes"	Two—both through a barnlike structure
Other noted elements	Themed storm-simulated launch with fog effects, elevated spiral, S-curve element, two crossovers with The Voyage
Top speed	60 mph
Ride time	1 minute, 18 seconds
Trains	Two 20-passenger B & M wing trains (five cars per train, four seats per car)
Cost	$22 million

That said, after we announced the kickoff and did the math, we realized we had miscounted. July 24 was 67 days after our first journal entry. We just acted as though we had planned that the whole time.

Announcement Day

At 5:00 a.m. on July 24, we kicked off our marathon day of media coverage for the announcement that would take place that night at closing time. Matt Eckert, Lauren, and I came armed with coffee and snacks to get us through the 17-hour day.

I'm not a great secret-keeper. I once blew a surprise party Dad was throwing for Mom *without actually knowing there was a surprise party.* Dad hadn't told me because he knew I'd blow it. And I still managed to ruin it.

I was nervous. We were all excited though. You could feel all around that this was going to be a game-changer. We gave media tours throughout the day. Lauren and I took a quick 20-minute catnap on our office floor. We rehearsed *that day* what we were going to say, and we were off.

Chad Benefield, a well-known radio emcee for WBKR in Owensboro, Kentucky, emceed the announcement without knowing what the ride even *was.* One thousand people gathered to watch the announcement in our Fireworks plaza, and the night felt electric. As the announcement ceremony ended, Paula shouted out "THUNDERBIRD! I CAN FINALLY SAY IT!" The excitement was so palpable—and it meant the world to us that we would open a B & M roller coaster five years after Dad passed.

Steel arrived the day after, and soon we were putting up the first pieces of track. And then we were topping the Immelmann element. And suddenly, the last piece of track was going in. As the piece went in, a contractor's radio nearby started playing "Come Together," by the Beatles, and I felt my dad—and his undying love of the Beatles—in that moment.

Will Power

The credit for the "Will Power" building at the ride goes to Chip Cleary, who served on our board of directors at the time we were developing Thunderbird—or, as we called the project at the time, BT15, which stood for Big Turkey 2015. Once we knew we were building a launch on the coaster, we had to figure out how to power it. Believe it or not, Santa Claus, Indiana, doesn't have a grid that will allow a massive draw of energy every 60 seconds or so. Building the launch meant that we needed flywheels to power the launch, and those flywheels needed their own building. PGAV Destinations recommended that we build the building in the plaza and very close to the rider clearance envelope to make the launch more thrilling on one side, as passing by at 60 miles per hour would feel VERY close.

At some point, Chip pointed out that the building should have a big "Will Power" sign on the side, and it stuck. Will Koch, the electrical engineer and coaster nerd, would be honored in a small way with a dedicated building to house the flywheels that powered our first major steel coaster.

But we didn't stop there. We honored our long-time employees in the queue as well. If you see a sign for Frieda's Flowers, that's for Frieda Foertsch, who held so many roles at the park, it's difficult to count. To name a few, she helped with the bird show, sewing Santa's costumes, and in her later years, taking care of the flowers and landscaping around the park. We

Facing, The last piece of track being lowered into place on Thunderbird. *Holiday World photo.*

Thunderbird's Will Power building is named as a tribute to Will Koch. *Holiday World photo.*

also honored Rick Emmons, our painter-turned-graphic-artist, who has designed almost every sign and logo you see in the park and painted the famous murals in Santa's Merry Marketplace, as well as our new "Santa Claus Land" mural on the side of the Skeeball building in the Christmas section. He's worked here for forty-six years. Tom Berg, a longtime carpenter and car enthusiast, has a sign up for his

The Koch and Crosby families celebrating the first launch of Thunderbird. *From left*, William Koch, Lauren Crosby, Lori Koch, and Leah Koch; *second row*, Michael Crosby. *Holiday World photo.*

"wagon business," and Richard Schwartz has a sign for his furniture-making hobby.

My favorite tribute is Hevron's Mercantile. It is named for Joe Hevron, who started working at Santa Claus Land in 1946 and stopping only to serve in the Korean War, after which he returned and worked until he was no longer able to work. I had the privilege of working with Joe in Cash Control for a few years in 2006–2009. He had a curmudgeonly exterior but a big heart. He cared deeply about the employees he hired, and he was known to show up

even on his days off. When we built Thunderbird just four years after he passed, we chose to name the store after Joe—an honor I'm sure he would have declared "too much," while sharing it with everyone he knew.

Saying Goodbye to an Attraction

In 2013, as our maintenance team was de-winterizing our attractions, the news hit: the Freedom Train, our longest-running attraction, would not open that year. The train had grown increasingly difficult to repair

through the years—parts were nearly impossible to find, and the train was more than sixty-five years old. When the maintenance technicians checked it, they said the engine had essentially crumbled over the winter. We had no choices left.

There were a few goodbyes that stung through the years. My siblings and I had never forgiven Dad for removing the Banshee, even though it was unreliable. We've said goodbye to Paul Revere's Midnight Ride, a "Monster" ride—and at the all-important entrance to Splashin' Safari, we also said goodbye to our original "Phase 1" of the water park: AmaZoom & Bamboo Chute, the Congo River, and Crocodile Isle. We said goodbye to Pilgrim's Plunge in 2014 because of its general lack of reliability.

When we add a ride, it becomes part of our family, and we know it becomes part of our visitors' families as well. It's never an easy decision to close one, and it often breaks our hearts.

The Freedom Train was the first and most difficult of these, and we dedicate ourselves now to maintaining those classic rides for as long as we can for that reason.

That said, we're also thrilled when we can say hello to a ride that previously seemed beyond repair. In 2016, we purchased a Calypso ride. It ran at LeSourdsville Lake Amusement Park near Cincinnati from 1972 until 2002, when the park closed permanently. The ride was then moved to Fun Spot in northeast Indiana, which closed in 2008. It had sat dormant since.

Our unparalleled maintenance team was up to the task at hand, and they restored the classic Calypso

Above, The Freedom Train faithfully served Holiday World for 65 years. *Holiday World photo.*

Left, The removal of the Freedom Train was a difficult decision for the Koch family (*from left*, Leah, Lauren, William, Will, and Lori). *Eric Photographic photo.*

ride. The paint shop added an automobile finish to make the cars sparkle, and we added a lighted sign for good measure. We named the ride "Firecracker" after the coaster that had resided in the 4th of July section years before.

Meet Kitty Claws

2012 kicked off a new era in Holiday World history: special events. Since Santafest had not proved successful in the late '80s and early '90s, we

Holiday World rescued and restored an abandoned Calypso ride in 2017. *Jim Futrell photo.*

avoided events and stuck to operating during our warm Indiana summers. But in 2012, we began an experiment that has changed our operating season entirely: Happy Halloween Weekends.

The event was designed to be the opposite of other Halloween attractions: specifically focused on the happy and fun elements of Halloween without the blood and gore. We planned to introduce a walk-through attraction, Holidog's 3-D Adventure Maze, and add a corn maze and a new Halloween show, decorate the park, and offer some nice fall foods.

To advertise the event, our team decided that our costume characters deserved a new addition, and Kitty Claws was born. In development, we knew that Holidog, George the Eagle, and Safari Sam needed a female companion, and a black cat seemed like a great fit for our spookiest holiday section. In the first drawings, her outfit was a little . . . lacking. We requested a tutu, and the rest was history—Kitty Claws is now as beloved as Holidog. And that's saying something.

Our Happy Halloween Weekends have made a huge difference in our "shoulder season" (off peak) attendance, and it's a great perk for our season passholders. Since 2012, we've expanded our event, added more fall treats, and added two more walk-through attractions: Carnival Chaos and SCAREbnb. And of course, Kitty Claws is still the star of the event!

The Renaissance of Wooden Coaster Maintenance

There's an adage in the attractions industry that everyone cites: you rebuild a wooden roller coaster every 10 years or so. It's true in some ways, but not in others. When off-season repairs come along, a wooden coaster team often finds itself repairing the most dynamic elements year after year. That's where we found ourselves in 2015.

The Legend is my favorite of our wooden roller coasters. In the park, we call it my "sister coaster." It's a long story that I'll try to summarize succinctly: my dad built three wooden coasters and had three children. At some point, The Legend became the apparent "middle child" of the coasters—it does a lot of heavy lifting and helped anchor our reputation for building the best wooden coasters in the world. However, it never won a number-one spot like The Raven and The Voyage did, and it didn't ever seem to draw in the attention or love that the first and third wooden coasters did. And somehow it became true: Lauren's coaster was The Raven, William's was The Voyage, and mine was The Legend.

When rumor caught that the coaster team wanted to do more than the standard off-season repairs on The Legend, I was elated. By the end of 2015, it was decided that we would close the attraction early and do something we had never done before: *smoothing*.

That year, we worked with Great Coasters International to help with the off-season maintenance and engineer the smoothing. Normally, the company works backward on a coaster, but the first drop and early elements of The Legend were the spots that needed the most improvement, so they made an exception.

The Legend Reborn project emerged in 2016. We replaced and smoothed all eight layers of track on the first drop, as well as the track after the double helix. When we made the smoothing changes, we also added a double up, double down element, and a tunnel around the Frightful Falls cross-under.

I was proud to see my sister coaster getting the love it always deserved during the summer of 2016, and We. Were. Hooked.

We've taken on several similar smoothing projects every year since, because they make the wooden coasters so much more comfortable. Since 2016, The Legend has had a second year of intensive work, and The Voyage has had two years of work on the "spaghetti bowl" and the "return track." In the 2020–2021 off-season, we worked with The Gravity Group to smooth out The Raven's "lake turn" and another turn toward the end of the course.

The best part of our smoothing projects is that the subtle engineering changes keep our most dynamic elements just as dynamic, but since the train moves more smoothly through the track, the repairs needed each off-season are reduced, freeing up our team to work on the smaller issues, and it brings our overall ride quality up.

I feel confident declaring that our wooden coasters are now among the best-maintained in the industry. Our team knows its next three years of coaster projects at any given point in time, and they're always reassessing, because they know better than anyone that wooden coasters still contain surprises.

That's why we like wooden coasters so much: they're alive, and maintaining them is a mix of proven science and a little bit of art. Depending on the temperature outdoors and the humidity, the ride can change as the wood expands and contracts. It's a dying art for many parks, and we want to make sure ours are ready to stand the test of time.

Facing, Leah Koch considers The Legend to be her "sister coaster." *Holiday World photo.*

Orange You Glad We Built Again?

I wish I could say it's not cool to have ride manufacturers specifically pitch new ideas to you to build in your own theme park, but it's EXACTLY as cool as it sounds.

Rick Hunter from ProSlide is the perfect example of the manufacturer who loves to dream of what Splashin' Safari can be, and he's always got a new project to pitch—and another ride concept in the works after that.

In the summer of 2018, another proposal from Rick was on the table. Maybe it's the fact that Canadians are the only people nicer than Hoosiers, but I just enjoy talking to Rick and hearing his energy and enthusiasm for the ProSlide show park. He had been talking about a Rocket-style water coaster for us to round out our collection.

Eventually, the idea stuck with our team. Much like with Thunderbird, we asked for a way to make this a new experience—after all, our guests were already familiar with two of the greatest water park rides in the world? How could Cheetah Chase make an interesting and new statement in Splashin' Safari?

It sounds a little like the story of Thunderbird: the launch came out of a conversation on how we could create a different ride experience for our guests. The name fell into place quickly: we knew we needed another animal to fit with Wildebeest and Mammoth, and we needed to convey the launch and the race at once. Cheetah Chase was born relatively easily out of that. Lauren worked with ProSlide on the color scheme, and we landed back at orange for a primary color.

For those of you who take issue with the "launched" water coaster, I'll agree with you a little. I, as the brand new director of communications— Paula retired in June 2019, and I stepped in—wanted to call Cheetah Chase the world's first flat-launched water coaster. There's a reason I'm not paid to be in

marketing. We often describe the linear induction motors on Wildebeest and Mammoth as giving a "launch" feeling as you are carried forward, so I felt "flat launch" was a fair way to describe it as the different experience it is (and in the process of reviewing other water coasters, we found a truly launched water coaster, but it was on an incline).

In 2020, we were set to open the ride in the second week of May when the world shut down due to the COVID pandemic. Our team worked from home, and those whose work happens entirely onsite stayed home. We decided early that our full-time team would be taken care of—no layoffs and no pay cuts. And we got on the phone with Indiana state government to let them know that it takes weeks, if not months, to open a theme park after it's been closed. They listened: Indiana's reopening plan set clear guidance for when amusement parks and water parks could reopen, and just like that, we were the first park in the country with an opening date in 2020. We made the best decisions we could, and our team pulled together in a way I hadn't seen before.

We decided early that Cheetah Chase would open in 2020, even though our gut feeling was that our guests had already decided whether they were going to visit, and it wasn't based on our new attraction. That said, we decided that keeping it closed for an attendance boost in another season felt wrong to us. And so, we opened Cheetah Chase—and it became an instant family favorite.

What Does the Future Look like?

This is a question we get a lot. We're a mature park now, as we learned when Thunderbird didn't grow our annual attendance the same way The Voyage did. We're also a 75-year-old park and we have 75-year-old buildings to maintain, and we still have plenty of rides from the '70s. We do our best not to discard old rides, but sometimes that means we have

Thunderbird Plaza was considered the prototype for the new immersive environments that the latest generation of owners sought to create. *Holiday World photo.*

to bypass a new attraction to keep a few older ones in top shape.

There are many projects that aren't as interesting to most that are very important to us. For example, we built Safari Outpost and Wildebeestro in 2014. This gift shop and restaurant were just added conveniences for our guests, and they served a practical purpose: our water park gift shop was our biggest one financially but took up a tiny amount of space since the water park opened, and we needed more water park restaurant capacity. But those two spaces also meant a lot more to my family. If we ever had to critique our dad, we would generally do so on theming. When the ride ran over budget, the theming

was the first to get cut. Those two buildings were our first working with PGAV Destinations, and to us, they showed the world where we were headed. Those buildings are themed to *our* standards today.

When Thunderbird came along, PGAV helped us develop the buildings for the plaza area, but we had to figure out how to execute, and do so affordably. For example, we learned the siding for the barn could be purchased pre-weathered, but our talented team of painters figured out how to do it themselves. Every panel you see on that barn was painted by Holiday World painters. Lauren and one of our vice presidents, Eric Snow, went out to an Amish auction house to find wheels, crates, plows, and even the wagon for our

Santa's Merry Marketplace was a major transformation of Holiday World's oldest building. *Holiday World image.*

queue. We decided as a team that we were going to do the whole area the right way.

In 2019, we finally took on the project we had put off for far too long: revamping Kringle's Kafé. The restaurant had been cobbled together from part of the Christmas Dining Room and a few restaurants in between. It wasn't a good layout, and it wasn't terribly well themed. In order to give our largest restaurant in the park the attention and capacity it deserved, we moved our offices out and gutted the building that had been so many different spaces since 1946. In the process, we found a Lewis Sorenson mural, years upon years of plaster and walls, and so much more. In May of 2019, we opened Santa's Merry Marketplace, a stunning restaurant with all the murals from

Kringle's Kafé, complete with Sugarplum Scoop Shoppe and Candy Cane Confectionery.

The new restaurant and Thunderbird Plaza are our shining examples of things to come, just as Wildebeestro and Safari Outpost are signs of things to come.

Lauren, Mom, William, and I all believe that our rides and restaurants and sections all need to tell a story, and that's what we'll continue to do. After all, we are America's First Theme Park.

Past Meets Future

Lauren, William, and I appreciate the genius of the first three generations of this company. Without our great-grandfather, Louis J., and his vision, we

During the Santa's Merry Marketplace project, workers uncovered an original Lewis Sorensen mural dating back to the late 1940s. *Holiday World photo.*

wouldn't be here. Without Bill lobbying to move Interstate 64 closer and expanding the park into a world of many holidays instead of a land of one, we wouldn't be here. And without our father Will taking big risks on wooden coasters, a water park, and free unlimited soft drinks, we wouldn't be here.

The generations before us shape the way we see the park and the vision we have for it. When I think about how lucky we are to have come from such visionaries and brilliant thinkers, I feel like an enormous imposter. How do we live up to our forefathers' visions? We don't.

We're paving our own direction. It's informed by our past, but it's not dictated by the past. I have no way of knowing what Will or Bill or Louis J. would

have done today, but I choose to believe in what Lauren, William, and I will do that I hope one day will make our children and grandchildren proud.

Our direction is different. Lauren spends hours upon hours analyzing building materials, paint colors, and theming to make each new addition immersive and cohesive with the rest of the park. I could spend my days dreaming and building my vision for the town of Santa Claus, and for Holiday World. Our goal is to immerse our visitors in a way that visitors to America's First Theme Park deserve, and we're getting there one move at a time. Next time you notice a new color on a building, know that Lauren has been working hard to pick the right color to either blend the building with its surroundings or

Family-Owned Amusement Parks

The Soul of the Industry

For many people, the amusement park industry conjures up images of the large corporate theme park—Disney, Universal, Sea World, Six Flags. While today's corporate giants dominate in the attractions industry, its soul remains the family-owned amusement park. They represent not just a business but family heirlooms that pass from generation to generation, much like the multigenerational memories that they provide their guests.

Any business surviving seventy-five years within the same family is remarkable—just 13 percent of family businesses remain in the family for more than sixty years, while only 3 percent of family businesses make it to the fourth generation.

But among amusement parks, it's even more special. Today there are approximately four hundred operating amusement parks in the United States, and of that total, about sixty have been owned by the same family for more than one generation in which the family still has an active role in the leadership of the business.

Even among this select group, Holiday World is one of only five amusement parks in which the fourth or fifth generation plays an active role in the operation. The seventy-five-year ownership of the Koch family is the eighth-longest continuous ownership by the same family of any amusement park in the United States.

A recent aerial view shows how Holiday World has been transformed into a major theme park. When it opened in 1946, the entire park was largely confined to the area in the lower right corner. *Holiday World photo.*

As the sun sets behind Thunderbird and The Voyage, Holiday World rests easy knowing that the legacy of the Koch family continues. *Holiday World photo.*

make it pop. Look at Santa's Merry Marketplace and appreciate the battles she fought to preserve each detail and value engineer the rest to make the project perfect. Next time you're in Thunderbird Plaza, know that she took the time to go to an Amish auction house to procure those wheels, jugs, and plows. And know that it's really difficult to find barrels.

The next time we announce a new ride, know that I've been writing and rewriting the story behind that ride for years. And whatever we announce, know that we have overanalyzed it to pieces because we want it to be *perfect*.

Know that I've calculated exactly how many years we can go between marquee attractions, and how big of a boost we'll see when we unveil a new one. If something seems like an accident here, it probably isn't.

Most importantly, know that as long as my family is here, and as long as we hold ownership in these parks, we will continue to pour our hearts into this place. We love the history and the smell of campfire wafting over from Lake Rudolph, and we love the people who built it. Most importantly, we love the people who visit, and open their hearts to us to tell their own stories about the park and what it means to them.

We may prefer to stay behind the scenes for now, but know that we spend a lot of time talking about *your* experience in the park and how we can make it better each time. Whatever we choose, I can promise you that we will cut a lot before we cut theming. Whatever we choose, we'll take longer to deliberate and decide than any reasonable person would. Whatever we choose, know that it's with our biggest, most earnest hearts that we make our choices. And whatever we choose, know that it's for *you*.

Appendix A ══════════════════

The Holiday World Attractions Index
1946 to Present

· AmaZoom water slide—1993 to 2012, relocated to Lake Rudolph Campground & RV Resort

· Baby Eli Wheel kiddie ride—early 1960s to mid-1970s, manufactured by Eli Bridge Company

· Bahari River lazy river—2006 to present

· Bahari wave pool—2005 to present, built by Aquatic Development

· Bakuli water slide—2007 to present, manufactured by ProSlide Technology

· Bamboo Chute water slide—1993 to 2012, relocated to Lake Rudolph Campground & RV Resort

· Banshee Falling Star—1986 to 2002, manufactured by Chance Rides

· Bavarian Glass Blowers—early 1960s to 1990s

· Blitzen's Airplanes/Sky King kiddie ride—mid-1960s to 2010

· Bungee Jump—1992

· Butterfly Bay/Parrot Cove kiddie water play area—1994 to present

· Cheetah Chase water coaster—2020 to present, manufactured by ProSlide Technology

· Children's Roller Coaster—early 1960s to late 1960s, manufactured by the Allan Herschell Company

· Cloud Nine/Moonwalk kiddie ride—1975 to late 1970s

· Comet's Rockets/North Star Sky Fighter—1970s to present, manufactured by the Allan Herschell Company

· Congo River lazy river—1993 to 2012

· Crocodile Isle children's splash area—1993 to 2012

· Crow's Nest/Sparkler tower swing—2012 to present, manufactured by Zamperla, replaced Paul Revere's Midnight Ride, moved from 4th of July to Thanksgiving in 2015

· Dancer's Thunder Bumpers Jr. kiddie bumper boats—1983 to 2013, manufactured by Webber Engineering, replaced Good Ship Lollipop; planned relocation to Splashin' Safari in 2014 did not occur

· Dancer's Fish/Salmon Run/Jonah's Whale Ride kiddie ride—1975 to present, manufactured by Eyerly Aircraft Company, relocated from 4th of July to Christmas in 2014

- Dasher's Seahorses/Neptune's Ponies kiddie ride—1965 to present

- Deer Farm/Animal Farm—1948 to 1976

- Deer Playground kiddie play area—1992 to 2007

- Doggone Trail Jeep Ride—1999 to present, manufactured by Zamperla

- Duck and Goose kiddie ride—early 1960s to mid-1970s, manufactured by the Allan Herschell Company

- Eagle's Flight Flying Scooters—1977 to present, manufactured by Bisch Rocco

- Educated Animal shows—mid-1960s to mid-1970s

- Enchanted Forest Trail/Fairyland Trail walk through storybook trail—1946 to late 1950s

- Firecracker Calypso—2017 to present, purchased from Fun Spot Amusement Park, Angola, Indiana, closed 2008; previously operated at Americana Amusement Park, Monroe, Ohio, 1972 to 2002

- Firecracker/Blitzen Roller Coaster—1981 to 1997, manufactured by Pinfari, purchased from Geauga Lake, Aurora, Ohio; sold to Jolly Roger Amusement Park, Ocean City, Maryland

- Freedom Train/Mother Goose Land Train/Fairyland Railroad/Santa Claus Land Railroad—1947 to 2012

- Frightful Falls Flume—1984 to present, manufactured by O. D. Hopkins

- Frontier Farm petting zoo—1977 to 2000, replaced the Deer Ranch

- German Band—1958 to 1978

- Giraffica/Pilgrim's Plunge Hyper Splash shoot-the-chutes—2009 to 2013, manufactured by Intamin Amusement Rides

- Gobbler Getaway dark ride—2006 to present, manufactured by Sally Dark Rides/Bertazzon

- Good Ship Lollipop/Kiddie Boats kiddie ride—1965 to early 1980s

- Hall of Famous Americans wax museum—1953 to 2002

- Hallow Swings swing ride—2003 to present, manufactured by Zamperla

- Handcars kiddie ride—1957 to mid-1970s, manufactured by Harold Chance

- Holidog Express Train—2013 to present, manufactured by Chance Rides

- Holidog's Treehouse play area—1999 to present

- House of Dolls/Betsy Ross Doll House—1947 to 2011, original Santa Claus post office relocated to the park, then moved to Santa Claus Park

- Howler roller coaster—1999 to present, manufactured by Zamperla

- Hyena Falls water slide—2013 to 2019, manufactured by ProSlide Technology

- Hyena Springs water play area—2013 to 2019

- Indian Village—1957 to early 1980s

- Jeep-Go-Round kiddie ride—1947 to late 1960s

- Jet Planes kiddie ride—early 1960s to late 1960s
- Jungle Jets sprayground—2004 to 2010, built by Waterworks International
- Jungle Racer water slide—2004 to present, manufactured by ProSlide Technology
- Just for Pups playground—1999 to present
- Kiddie Boats kiddie ride—1940s to mid-1960s
- Good Ship Lollipop/Kiddie Boats kiddie ride—1965 to early 1980s
- Kiddie Train kiddie ride—1946 to late 1960s
- Kid's Castle—1992 to 2007
- Kima Bay waterplay area—2008 to present, manufactured by Whitewater West Industries
- Kitty's Tea Party teacups—2013 to present, manufactured by Zamperla
- Lewis and Clark Trail antique autos—1978 to present, manufactured by Gould Manufacturing
- Liberty Launch drop tower—2003 to present, manufactured by S & S Power, replaced Hall of Famous Americans
- Lincoln Display—early 1950s to early 1980s
- Magic Waters spray ground—1999 to present
- Mammoth water coaster—2012 to present, manufactured by ProSlide Technology
- Mayflower swinging ship—2014 to present, manufactured by Chance Rides
- Merry-Go-Round—early 1960s to late 1960s, manufactured by the Allan Herschell Company
- Miniature Circus—1950 to late 1970s, built by the Colvin family
- Monsoon Lagoon water play area—1998 to 2018, manufactured by SCS Interactive
- Nativity—1947 to present
- Otorongo water slide—1997 to present, manufactured by ProSlide Technology
- Paul Revere's Midnight Ride Spider—1978 to 2011, manufactured by Eyerly Aircraft Company
- Pioneer Land Train—1957 to 1974
- Pioneer Land Train Tour Tram—1975 to early 1980s, manufactured by Chance Rides, replaced original Pioneer Land Train
- Pioneer Village—1957 to early 1980s
- Pow Wow/Spinning Drummer Tubs Of Fun—1975 to 1989, manufactured by Hampton Rides
- Prancer's Merry-Go-Round/All the King's Horses kiddie ride—mid-1970s to present
- Raging Rapids river rapids—1990 to present, manufactured by O. D. Hopkins
- Reindeer Games drop tower—2008 to present, manufactured by Moser Rides, replaced Kids Castle
- Revolution Round Up—2005 to present, manufactured by Dartron Industries
- River Boat Museum—1965 to late 1960s

- Rough Riders/Sunday Drivers bumper cars—1975 to present, cars replaced in 2001
- Round House/Arctic Circle Round Up—1976 to 2004, manufactured by Frank Hrubetz & Company, purchased from Buckeye Lake Amusement Park, Buckeye Lake, Ohio
- Rudolph's Round Up Sleighs kiddie ride—2011 to present, replaced Blitzen's Airplanes
- Safari Sam's Splashland water play area—2011 to present, replaced Jungle Jets
- Indian Dance/Snow Swirl Whip kiddie ride—1975 to 1991, manufactured by W. F. Mangels
- Scarecrow Scrambler/Reindeer Round Up Scrambler—1975 to present, manufactured by Eli Bridge Company, purchased from Mesker Park Rides, Evansville, Indiana
- Stagecoach—1957 to early 1960s, later displayed in Transportation Museum
- Star Spangled Carousel—2008 to present, manufactured by Chance Rides, replaced Thunder Bumpers
- Stars and Stripes Showdown—2015, manufactured by Skyline Attractions
- Street Car kiddie ride—1957 to late 1960s
- Stormin' Norman's Tank Tag—1992 to 1996, replaced Indian Dance kiddie whip
- Tembo Falls water slides—2018 to present, manufactured by ProSlide Technology
- Tembo Tides junior wave pool—2018 to present
- The Legend roller coaster—2000 to present, built by Custom Coasters
- The Raven roller coaster—1995 to present, built by Custom Coasters
- The Voyage roller coaster—2006 to present, built by The Gravity Group
- The Wave wave pool—1994 to present
- Thunder Bumpers bumper boats—1980 to 2007
- Thunderbird roller coaster—2015 to present, manufactured by Bolliger & Mabilliard
- Tippecanoes/Indian River Canoes kiddie ride—1990 to present, manufactured by Venture Manufacturing, replaced Pow Wow
- Toyland toy museum—1946 to 2010s
- Transportation Museum—1965 to 1976
- Turkey Whirl Tilt-A-Whirl—2007 to present, manufactured by Sellner Manufacturing
- Virginia Reel/Wynken, Blynken, and Nod Tilt-A-Whirl—1976 to 2005, purchased from Mesker Park Rides, Evansville, Indiana
- Water Ski Thrill Show—1959 to 1961
- Watubee water slide—1996 to present, manufactured by ProSlide Technology
- Wildebeest water coaster—2010 to present, manufactured by ProSlide Technology
- Zinga water slide—2003 to present, manufactured by ProSlide Technology
- Zoombabwe water slide—2002 to present, manufactured by ProSlide Technology

Appendix B

Holiday World & Splashin' Safari Awards and Accolades

About.com

Best New Water Park Ride—Wildebeest, 2011

Best New Water Park Ride—Mammoth, 2013

American Coaster Enthusiasts

ACE Roller Coaster Landmark—The Raven, 2016

Better Business Bureau

Business Integrity Award Winner, Category IV—Holiday World & Splashin' Safari, 2007

Centric Indiana

Innovation Award—Thunderbird, 2016

Coaster101

Park Mania Winner, 2020

Consumer's Digest

Best Value Park—2007, 2012, 2017

Ernst & Young

Entrepreneur of the Year—William A. Koch Jr., 2004

FamilyFun Magazine

Nation's #3 Amusement Park, 2013

Feedspot

Top 50 Theme Park Blogs, 2017, #16

Top 40 Theme Park Blogs and Websites to Follow, 2021, #11

Food Allergy & Anaphylaxis Network

Mariel C. Furlong Award for Making a Difference, 2009

Forbes American Heritage Magazine

Top 10 Coasters—The Raven, 1998

Golden Ticket Awards presented by *Amusement Today*

#1 Wooden Roller Coaster—The Raven, 2000–2003

#1 Wooden Roller Coaster—The Voyage, 2007–2011

Best New Ride—Amusement Park—The Voyage, 2006

Best New Ride—Water Park—Bahari River, 2006

Best New Ride—Water Park—Wildebeest, 2010

Best Water Park Ride—Zinga, 2003

Best Water Park Ride—Mammoth, 2012

Best Water Park—#2—Splashin' Safari, 2002–2018

Cleanest Park—2000–2018

Friendliest Park—1998–2008, 2010–2011

Legends Series—Will Koch, 2010

Publisher's Pick—Outstanding Customer Service, 2004

Guinness Book of World Records

Mammoth—World's Longest Water Coaster Certified, 2016

Home To Go

Most Affordable Theme Parks in America—2019, #2

Indiana Economic Development Corporation

Half Century Award—2021 Koch Development Corporation for 76 Years of Operation

Indiana Governor's Planning Council for People with Disabilities

Profit from our Abilities Statewide Award of Excellence, 2002

Indiana Ready Mixed Concrete Association

Outstanding Concrete Achievement Award, 2005

Indiana Tourism

Happy Halloween Weekends—Indiana's #1 Destination for Fall Family Fun, 2013; awarded by the Indiana Tourism Office

Happy Halloween Weekends—Best Event/Festival 2019; awarded by the Indiana Tourism Association

Will Koch Tourism Leadership Award, created in memory of Will Koch

Indiana University Kelley School of Business

Johnson Center for Entrepreneurship and Innovation 2005 Innovation Winner

Inside Track Readers Pool

Favorite Parks—1995, #5

Favorite Roller Coasters—Raven, 1995, #3

Favorite Water Parks—1995, #8

Friendliest Park Staff—1995, #1

Most Significant New Attraction—Raven, 1995, #1

International Association of Amusement Parks and Attractions (IAAPA)

Hall of Fame—Bill Koch, 2001

Hall of Fame—Will Koch, 2010

IAAPA Service Awards—Best Promotion, Free Unlimited Soft Drinks, 2000

Brass Ring Awards:

Brochure, Amusement /Theme Park with attendance from 250,001 to 500,000—1994, 3rd

Print Advertising, Amusement /Theme Park with attendance from 250,001 to 500,000—1994, 3rd

Radio, Amusement /Theme Park with attendance from 250,001 to 500,000—1994, 1st

Television Commercial, Amusement /Theme Park with attendance from 250,001 to 500,000—1994, 2nd; 1995, 2nd; 1996, 2nd

International Ride Training

Ride Operations Excellence Award—2017, 2018

Liseberg Park/Amusement Business

Applause Award—2004

Men's Journal

"Nation's 9 Top Coasters" The Voyage—2014

National Amusement Parks Historical Association Annual Members' Survey

Best New Attraction—The Raven 1995, The Voyage 2006

Best Park for Families—1999 (#5), 2000 (#4), 2001 (#3), 2002 (#3), 2004 (#5), 2005 (#2), 2006 (#4), 2007 (#3), 2008 (#3), 2009 (#4), 2010 (#4), 2011 (#2, tie), 2012 (#3)

Favorite Theme Park—2007 (#4, tie), 2008 (#3, tie), 2009 (#3), 2011 (#3),

Favorite Wooden Roller Coaster—The Raven 1995 (#5), 1998 (#3), 1999 (#4), 2001 (#3), 2003 (#5), 2004 (#4)
The Voyage 2006 (#2), 2007, (#1, tie), 2008 (#1), 2009 (#1), 2010 (#1), 2012 (#2), 2013 (#2), 2014 (#2)

People Magazine

"21 Amusement Park Foods From Across the Country that Everyone Needs to Try at Least Once": Holiday World Featured Foods: Festive Flurry and Full Thanksgiving Dinner

Popular Mechanics

The Voyage, Best Roller Coaster in Indiana, 2019

Real Simple Magazine

#1 Scare You Silly Coaster—The Voyage, 2007

Spencer County Regional Chamber of Commerce

Business of the Year Award—2021

Thrilling 32

The Voyage—Wooden Coaster Champion

Time Magazine

#1 Wooden Roller Coaster—2013

Travel Channel

"Most Insane" wooden roller coaster on "Insane Coaster Wars"— The Voyage, 2012

TripAdvisor

America's Top 10 Water Parks—2011, #1

Top Water Parks—2018, #5 in America, #15 in the World

TripAdvisor Hall of Fame—2019

Traveler's Choice Award

Splashin' Safari #1 Water Park in the Nation—2012

Splashin' Safari #4 Water Park in the Nation—2014

Splashin' Safari #3 Water Park in the Nation; #15 Water Park in the World—2015

Splashin' Safari #4 Water Park in the Nation; #13 Water Park in the World—2016

Splashin' Safari #4 Water Park in the Nation—2017

Splashin' Safari # 5 Water Park in the Nation—2018

Splashin' Safari #15 Water Park in the Nation—2020

Certificate of Excellence—2011, 2012, 2013, 2015, 2016, 2017, 2018, 2019

Hall of Fame—2019

USA Today 10 Best Poll

America's Best Outdoor Water Park—2013, 2017, 2019; ranked in Top 10 from 2015 to 2021

America's Best Roller Coaster—Top 10—2015, 2019, 2020

America's Best Amusement Park—2017, #4

America's Best New Amusement Park Attraction in 2015—Thunderbird, #4

America's Best New Amusement Park Attraction in 2020—Cheetah Chase, #3

Further Reading

Books

Hill, Barry, R. *Imagineering an American Dreamscape, Genesis, Evolution and Redemption of the Regional Theme Park*. Cary, IL: Rivershore Press, 2020.

Koch, Pat, and Jane Ammeson. *Images of America Holiday World*. Mount Pleasant, SC: Arcadia, 2006.

Kyrazi, Gary. *The Great American Amusement Parks*. Secaucus, NJ: Citadel, 1976.

Silverman, Stephen M. *The Amusement Park: 900 Years of Thrills and Spills and the Dreamers and Schemers Who Built Them*. New York: Black Dog & Leventhal, 2019.

Additional Resources

rcdb (Roller Coaster Database), www.rcdb.com

American Coaster Enthusiasts. "The Journey to The Voyage." *RollerCoaster!* 101, vol. 28, no. 3 (Spring 2007).

About the Authors

Jim Futrell—Editor, Chapters 2 and 3

Jim Futrell's passion for amusement parks was ignited in the 1970s when a neighbor who worked in public relations for a theme park under development near his native Chicago, gave him leftover publicity materials.

In 1980, he joined the National Amusement Parks Historical Association (NAPHA) and has served at that organization's historian since 1984. Jim has spent more than 40 years documenting the industry, authoring more than seventy articles for industry trade publications along with dozens for the NAPHA Chronicle. His first book, an amusement park directory, was released in 1990. It has been followed by seven additional books on the industry. He has been quoted more than one hundred fifty times in other publications and made ten national television appearances.

Jim is also involved with the International Association of Amusement Parks and Attractions (IAAPA), serving on the Hall of Fame Committee and as historian. He heads up the organization's oral history project and compiled their official centennial history. His efforts resulted in him being presented with the association's Outstanding Service Award in 2018.

Jim has visited nearly 500 different amusement parks and ridden more than 700 roller coasters.

Ron Gustafson—Recollections, Chapter 5

Ron Gustafson is an award-winning journalist and photojournalist who has covered the industry for nearly fifty years. His work has been published in trade journals, magazines, and newspapers worldwide. His two books highlight the history of trolley parks and ride manufacturers in the United States. He has served as marketing and public relations director at Quassy Amusement & Waterpark in Middlebury, Connecticut, as well as the former Midway Amusement Park in Maple Springs, New York. His marketing materials have won numerous Brass Ring Awards from the IAAPA as well as two Best Promotion of the Year honors. Ron has volunteered on a number of IAAPA committees over the years and chaired its Hall of Fame committee 2012–2014. In addition, he is newsletter editor for NEAAPA—the Northeast's Entertainment Association. He and his wife Nancy have two grown children and two grandsons.

Dave Hahner—Chapter 4

Dave Hahner has been a huge fan of amusement parks and roller coasters for his entire life. Growing up not far from Kennywood Park near Pittsburgh, Pennsylvania, Dave worked summers at the park in his youth. While working at the park, he met members of American Coaster Enthusiasts (ACE) and quickly joined. More than 40 years later, Dave is just as enamored with rides and amusement parks, big and small. He wrote a book on the history of Kennywood in 2004 and became historian for ACE a few years later. While historian, he helped to write several ACE Roller Coaster Landmark plaques including the one for The Raven. He has written several historical articles on amusement parks and roller coasters over the years for ACE and other enthusiast organization publications. His work includes a book he coauthored with Jim Futrell on the now-defunct Geauga Lake amusement near Cleveland, Ohio. Dave and his family love to travel to various amusement parks across the country, but among their favorites has always been Holiday World.

Nell Hedge—Chapter 1

Nell Hedge is executive director of the Santa Claus Museum & Village in Santa Claus, Indiana. The Santa Claus Museum & Village is dedicated to the preservation and interpretation of the history of Santa Claus, Indiana, and it perpetuates the tradition of Santa's Elves, Incorporated, by answering letters to Santa. She graduated from Indiana University with a bachelor's degree in tourism management and has experience in education, communications, and community outreach. Nell was named to the position in 2018.

Leah Koch—Chapter 6

Leah Koch represents the fourth generation of Koch family members to own and operate Holiday World & Splashin' Safari. Like many family operators, Leah began working in seasonal positions as a teen in a variety of jobs in Foods, Cash Control, Entertainment, Rides, and Public Relations. She joined the company's board of directors in 2013 and in 2014 became the park's director of research and development where she collaborated with consultants to develop 5-, 10-, and 20-year strategic plans for park growth. Leah became director of communications in 2019. She graduated from Indiana University's Kelley School of Business MBA program, where she majored in business analytics and corporate innovation.